URIEL

About the Author

Richard Webster is the author of more than thirty books published by Llewellyn during the past decade, as well as many others published in New Zealand and elsewhere. A resident of New Zealand, he travels extensively, giving workshops, seminars, and lectures on the topics of which he writes.

COMMUNICATING WITH
THE ARCHANGEL

URIEL

FOR TRANSFORMATION
& TRANQUILITY

Richard Webster

Llewellyn Publications
Woodbury, Minnesota

First Edition
Fourth Printing, 2008
Cover design by Gavin Dayton Duffy
Cover illustration © 2004 by Neal Armstrong / Koralik & Associates
Edited by Andrea Neff
Series design by Michael Maupin

Llewellyn is a registered trademark of Llewellyn Worldwide, Ltd.

Library of Congress Cataloging-in-Publication Data

Webster, Richard.
    Uriel : communicating with the Archangel for transformation & tranquil-
ity / Richard Webster.—1st ed.
        p.   cm.
    Includes bibliographical references and index.
    ISBN 13: 978-0-7387-0703-7
    ISBN 10: 0-7387-0703-1
    1. Uriel (Archangel)—Miscellanea. I. Title.

    BL477.W44 2005
    202'.15—dc22   2005044108

Llewellyn Publications
A Division of Llewellyn Worldwide, Ltd.
2143 Wooddale Drive
Woodbury, MN 55125-2989, U.S.A.
www.llewellyn.com

Printed in the United States of America

The Archangels Series
by Richard Webster

Gabriel

Michael

Raphael

Uriel

Also available in Spanish

Also by Richard Webster

For my good friends
Moshe and Tova Botwinick.
Your prediction was correct!

CONTENTS

Introduction

THE word *angel* is derived from the Greek word *angelos*, which itself comes from the Hebrew word *mal'akh*, meaning "messenger." This shows that since ancient times the angels' most important role is to act as messengers between God and mankind.

I find it interesting to ask people what they imagine angels to be like. Naturally, many people visualize them as cute cherubs with wings, but others see them as giant-like, powerful, even slightly intimidating beings. When I was a child, an elderly friend of my mother told me that angels were like shadows with auras around them. She also said that magicians and witches were able to draw energy from these shadows to do their work.

Not long ago, one lady surprised me. She told me that she saw angels as everyday people, but with special qualities that were usually not apparent until after they had left. This made me recall the haunting words from Hebrews 13:2: "Be not forgetful to entertain strangers: for thereby some have entertained angels unawares." She also said that in her experience, angels usually appeared when the person desperately needed help or encouragement. The American poet John Greenleaf Whittier (1807–92) must have agreed with her when he wrote:[1]

> With silence only as their benediction God's angels come, Where, in the shadow of a great affliction, the soul sits dumb.

People visualize angels in different ways. This is not surprising, as angels have the ability to appear in any shape or form they wish, depending upon the circumstances. It makes no difference how you see them. In fact, you may even see them in a variety of forms at different times.

Communicating with angels has the potential to transform your life. All you have to do is invite them in. Once you do this, the angelic kingdom will nurture and encourage you at every stage of life. Angels are endlessly forgiving, caring, and supportive. They provide strength, healing, light, energy, and healing.

The history of angels is a fascinating one that in the Christian tradition goes back to the first day of creation. In the book of Jubilees, one of the apocryphal religious texts that was excluded from the Bible, angels are said to have been created on the first day, after the heavens and earth, but before the firmament. This meant that angels were able to help God with his creation.

Intriguingly, the book of Genesis makes no mention of this. The first mention of an angel in the Bible is when the angel of the Lord appeared to Hagar, a young, pregnant serving girl, who was fleeing from Abram's wife, Sarai. (Genesis 16:7). The "angel of the Lord" appears frequently in the Old Testament. This angel engaged Hagar in conversation, and said: "Return to thy mistress and submit thyself under her hands." (Genesis 16:9) The angel of the Lord also told her that she would give birth to a son named Ishmael.

The first biblical reference to the creation of angels is in the book of Job (38:4–7). In this reference, angels are called "sons of God":

> Where was thou when I laid the foundations of the earth? declare, if thou hast understanding. Who hath laid the measures thereof, if thou knowest? or who hath stretched the line upon it? Whereupon are the foundations thereof fastened? or who laid the cornerstone thereof, when the morning stars sang together, and all the sons of God shouted for joy?

The next mention of the creation of angels is in Psalm 148, verses 1–5:

> Praise ye the Lord. Praise ye the Lord from the heavens: praise him in the heights. Praise ye him, all his angels: praise ye him all his hosts. Praise ye him, sun and moon: praise him all ye stars of light. Praise him, ye heavens of heavens, and ye waters that be above the

heavens. Let them praise the name of the Lord: for he commanded, and they were created.

Saint Paul refers to God's creation of angels in his Epistle to the Colossians (1:16):

For by him were all things created, that are in heaven, and that are in earth, visible and invisible, whether they be thrones, or dominions, or principalities, or powers: all things were created by him, and for him.

Thrones, dominions, principalities, and powers are all groupings of angels. There are different arrangements of these, known as hierarchies. The one that is generally accepted was devised by Pseudo-Dionysius, a fifth- or sixth-century writer and philosopher. According to him, there are nine groups of angels. At the top are the Seraphim, the angels closest to God. These are followed in descending order by the Cherubim, Thrones, Dominions, Virtues, Powers, Principalities, Archangels, and Angels.[2]

Angels have also figured in every other major religious tradition. Carved stone cylinder seals, dating from about 4000 BCE, have been found in Ur, the capital city of the ancient Sumerians. The cylinders show a man and a god. Next to the man is another figure who appears to be leading him to the god. This person is probably an angel, even though he does not have wings.

Arguably, the first picture of an angel is an engraved stone panel from Sumeria. The engraving depicts a king catching drops of the water of life that is being spilled from a container held by a winged figure, presumably an angel.

In ancient Egypt, angels were called the Shining Ones. They painted and sculpted angels in tombs and temples. The inscrutable Sphinx of Giza is a huge example, and is a monument to their great angel Hu.[3]

Followers of the Iranian prophet Zoroaster (c. 628–551 BCE) believed in *amesha spentas,* who appeared to be angels of Ahura Mazda, the Wise Lord. If not true angels, they were certainly intermediary beings who functioned in both heaven and earth. Zoroaster had a life-changing experience at the age of thirty when he experienced a vision of the Archangel of Right Thinking, who was about nine times the size of a human being. Zoroaster was so moved by this experience that he stepped out of his physical body and came immediately into the presence of God, who he called "Lord of Light." God taught Zoroaster everything he needed to know to start his religion. For several years, Zoroaster was also assisted and taught by the Immortal Holy Ones, who were six archangels. He was introduced to many other angels, and discovered that there was a Lord of Light, as well as a Lord of Darkness, who had an army of demons to help him. These concepts were later adopted by many other religions, especially Judaism and Christianity.

In Islam, the Archangel Gabriel revealed the Koran to Muhammad. In Islam there are three types of spiritual beings: angels, demons, and *jinn*, or genies. According to legend, the jinn were created two thousand years before Adam, and can work either negatively or positively, according to the situation they find themselves in. They are inclined to be mischievous and frequently make life difficult for the people they torment and tease. Fortunately, it is possible to outwit them using superior thought, cunning, or magic.

In Judaism, angelology became more developed during their time of exile (fifth and sixth centuries BCE), when they made contact with followers of Zoroastrianism. The army of hosts that developed during this time actively fight the forces of evil, and perform other tasks, such as revealing the word of God to mankind. Jewish Kabbalists also related angels to the four elements, and arranged them into a hierarchy.

The four leading archangels became well-known during this period. Michael is the warrior leader of the heavenly hosts, while Gabriel performs the role of heavenly messenger. Both of them are mentioned by name in the canonical Old Testament. Raphael, God's healer, is mentioned in the book of Tobit, and Uriel, the Fire of God, is recognized in 2 Esdras. A Jewish evening prayer also includes all four archangels:

> May Michael, the protector of God, stand at my right hand; and Gabriel, the power of God, stand at my left; before me, Uriel, the light of God; and behind me, Raphael, the healing of God. And above my head, may there be the abiding presence of God, the Shekinah.

The book of Genesis (28:12–16) describes Jacob's dream. He dreamed of a ladder leading from earth to heaven, with angels walking up and down it. This dream describes the cosmic link between heaven and earth, and has also been used to explain how angels were able to travel between the different sephiroth, the areas of divine attributes, in the Kabbalistic Tree of Life.

Over the last two thousand years, the Christian church has endlessly debated the nature and attributes of angels. The chubby, benign cherubic figures that are the popular ideal of angels are the creation of the Church, and have little in common with the powerful angels that appear in the Bible and other holy books.

The first Ecumenical Council in 325 CE acknowledged the existence of angels. The council went so far as to state that Christians could ask angels to help them get to heaven. However, the second council, less than twenty years later, contradicted this because it felt that adoration of angels would confuse people and take them away from the worship of Christ. It was not until 787 CE that the Seventh Ecumenical Synod announced that angels were intermediaries who could intercede between God and man. This synod also adopted the Celestial Order proposed by Pseudo-Dionysius, and this has created confusion ever since.

In the Middle Ages, Thomas Aquinas (1225–74) suggested that angels were composed of pure spirit, but could assume physical form whenever necessary. Thomas Aquinas had a huge influence on Christian thinking, and in his major work, *Summa Theologica*, answered 118 specific questions about angels.

The multi-talented Swedish scientist and mystic Emanuel Swedenborg (1688–1772) wrote many books of theology with the help and guidance of the angels he conversed with every day. His writings are still available and, despite a number of contradictions,[4] provide detailed descriptions of his view of the angelic kingdom.

In more recent times, the Swiss theologian Karl Barth (1886–1968) conducted valuable research into angels. He believed that angels bring heaven down to earth. When they speak to us, it is actually God talking to us. When they act, it is actually God acting. Karl Barth felt that angels were above us because they could witness God at work. However, at the same time, he felt that they were below us, because God's work was directed towards people rather than the angelic kingdom. Karl Barth wrote: "To deny the angels is to deny God himself."[5]

There is no doubt that research into angels will continue as long as humans inhabit the earth. New ideas are proposed all the time. One example came from Dr. Geddes MacGregor, Emeritus Distinguished Professor of Philosophy at the University of Southern California, who suggested that angels may be a highly evolved race of extraterrestrials.[6]

However, along with the ongoing research, a growing number of people are discovering angels in their own way, and are establishing personal connections with them. This valuable development has enormous implications, because angels can see what lies ahead of us, and can guide us accordingly. Angels also enable us to understand and realize that we are part of God, and are here to undertake a divine mission. Working with angels is a transforming experience.

It is likely to change your perceptions about every aspect of your life.

In the next chapter, we will start to learn about Uriel, one of the four great archangels.

One

WHO IS URIEL?

UNLIKE Michael, Gabriel, and Raphael, Uriel is not mentioned by name in the canonical scriptures. However, as you will see, he is at least as important as the other archangels. The name Uriel means "God is my light" or "Fire of God." Uriel received this name because he taught the Torah to Moses, revealing to him the evils of sin.

In the first book of Enoch, Uriel is described as one of the holy angels who keep watch over humanity. He is in charge of thunder and earthquakes (Enoch 20:2). In the book of Adam and Eve, he is in charge of repentance.

According to the *Apocalypse of Moses,* Uriel and Michael were the two angels who buried Adam in heaven. However, the Zohar says that three angels are present at the deathbed of everyone. It seems that Gabriel must have been employed elsewhere at the time of Adam's death. However, a number of texts describe Adam's burial, and they all mention different numbers of angels in attendance.[1]

Although Uriel is not mentioned by name in the Bible, he is believed to be the angel of the Lord who destroyed the hosts of Sennacherib (II Kings 19:35). Uriel is also believed to be the angel who wrestled with Jacob for a full night (Genesis 32:24–32). This story is a fascinating one, as it shows that sometimes our struggles with Uriel are on a one-to-one basis, as he tries to bring us closer to God. In the account in Genesis, Jacob sent away his two wives, women servants, and eleven sons, which showed his willingness to eliminate most of the external things that stood in the way of a closer connection with God. However, there were still inner obstacles to be dealt with, and this is why Jacob wrestled with an angel for a full night.

Enlightenment can be related to the start of the new day. At this point, Uriel said, "Let me go, for the day breaketh." Jacob replied, "I will not let thee go, except thou bless me." Uriel then asked Jacob what his name was. When Jacob told him, he symbolically gave up all resistance and gained a oneness with God. Uriel was satisfied at last, and said: "Thy name shall be called no more Jacob, but Israel: for as a prince hast thou power with God and with men, and hast prevailed."

In Jewish legend, it was Uriel who warned Noah of the flood. This is recounted in the book of Enoch (1:1–3). Uriel is also a highly gifted teacher. He was Enoch's guide and teacher throughout most of his tour of the heavens. He is believed to have taught Seth, Adam's son, the mysteries of astronomy, time, and Hebrew characters.[2] He also taught Ezra that evil has a certain amount of time to run its course. Ezra found this hard to understand, and Uriel arranged for him to have seven prophetic dreams to help explain the matter. These dreams covered the entire course of human history up to that time, and beyond. Uriel helped him interpret and understand the messages in the dreams.[3]

Another Hebrew legend tells how Uriel was involved in the burial of Abel. Apparently, after Cain killed Abel, he tried to bury him, but the earth would not accept the body, and kept bringing it back to the surface. Uriel, Michael, Gabriel, and Raphael saw this and, when Cain fled, took Abel's body and placed it on a rock, where it lay for many years without decomposing.

In the apocryphal second book of Esdras,[4] Uriel rebuked and shamed the prophet for assuming too much about the ways of God. Esdras reproached God for helping Israel's enemies. Uriel, who was travelling with Esdras, replied that he would reveal God's reasons after the prophet had weighed fire, measured the wind, and brought back the previous day. Esdras said that he could do none of those things. Uriel then said that if Esdras knew the fire, wind, and days, but could not understand them, how could he possibly understand God's intentions, when he did not know Him? Esdras immediately fell at Uriel's feet and asked for forgiveness.

In the *Sibylline Oracles*,[5] Uriel is mentioned as the angel who looks after the keys to hell, and is waiting to open the gates on Judgment Day. Consequently, Uriel punishes sinners when necessary, but is also more than willing to help people who need it.

Uriel in Literature

Uriel also appears in literature. Michael, Gabriel, Raphael, and Uriel all appear in the epic poem *Paradise Lost* by John Milton (1608–74), which was printed in 1667. In *Paradise Lost,* one of the greatest poems in the English language, John Milton described Uriel as being the "sharpest sighted spirit in all of heaven."

Consequently, it is rather surprising that in book III of the poem, Satan was able to fool Uriel when he transformed himself into a cherub and tricked the archangel into telling him where Adam and Eve lived. When Uriel discovered what he had done, he told Gabriel, who was guarding the Garden of Eden, to be on the look out for the devil. Two angels were placed close beside Adam and Eve to protect them. Satan turned himself into a cricket, and whispered an evil message into Eve's ear. Gabriel managed to find Satan, who refused to say what he had been up to, and flew back to hell.[6] Uriel was extremely distressed at having been fooled by Satan, and blamed himself for what had happened. He told God that he would guard the gates of hell for all time, as a penance for his mistake, and to exercise vengeance on evildoers. In some of the early religious texts, hell was ruled by avenging angels rather than Satan. *The Apocalypse of Saint Peter* gives a detailed account of the punishments meted out to sinners under the leadership of Uriel.

In his play *The State of Innocence, and Fall of Man* (1677), John Dryden (1631–1700) has Uriel descend from heaven in a chariot drawn by four white horses. This play was a dramatized version of *Paradise Lost.*

In May 1798, Charles Lamb (1775–1834) wrote a letter to his friend, the poet Samuel Taylor Coleridge (1772–1834), posing a series of theological questions largely concerning the angelic kingdom. The second question was: "Whether the Archangel Uriel *could* affirm an untruth? And if he *could,* whether he *would?*"[7]

Uriel in Music

Uriel also plays a role in Franz Joseph Haydn's famous oratorio *The Creation,* which was first performed in 1798. Haydn based his work on *Paradise Lost.* Uriel announces the famous words from Genesis: "And God saw the light, that it was good . . . And God said, Let there be lights in the firmament of the heaven, to divide the day from the night . . . to give light upon the earth, and it was so . . . He made the stars also." (Genesis 1:4–16)

Uriel in Art

Uriel appears rarely in religious art, compared to Michael, Gabriel, and Raphael. He is normally shown carrying a scroll and a book, and in the company of the other archangels. He is sometimes depicted with a flame burning in the palm of one hand. This signifies God's love for humanity, and also illuminates the world so that we can see the beauty that surrounds us in God's creation. Artists normally show Uriel as a man in his forties, with dark, curly hair, and usually with a beard. Michael, Gabriel, and Raphael are never shown with beards. Most of the time, Uriel wears green or brown clothing, as these colors relate to the earth element.

In 1483, the Confraternity of the Immaculate Conception commissioned Leonardo da Vinci to produce the central painting of a triptych intended for the altar of their chapel in Milan. What is interesting about this commission is the detailed specifications that were given to the artist. The original contract still survives, and gives the exact specifications of the painting. This was not surprising, as the altar already existed and the painting had to fit into a certain space. However, the contract also specified what needed to be included in the painting. The painting had to depict a legendary story that was not mentioned in the Gospels. This story says that during the flight to Egypt, Joseph, Mary, and Jesus took shelter in a desert cave. John the Baptist was already in the cave, with his protector, Archangel Uriel. The purpose of this meeting was to enable the infant Jesus to give John the Baptist the authority to baptize him when they were both adults. The reason for this legend is obvious. As Jesus was without sin, he technically did not need to be baptized at all. This legend appears to resolve what could otherwise be an embarrassing problem.

Leonardo painted two versions of this meeting, called *The Virgin of the Rocks.* One of these is in the Louvre, in Paris, and the other is in the National Gallery in London. The Louvre has another painting of Uriel called *Divine*

Vengeance and Justice by Prud'hon, and this depicts Uriel as the avenging angel.

As early as the fourth century CE, Christian fathers were becoming disturbed at the influence angels had on people, and believed that some people were worshiping them. Consequently, all angels, except for Michael, Gabriel, and Raphael, were banned at the Synod of Laodicea.

In the eighth century, the Christian fathers again became concerned at the number of people worshiping angels. Pope Zachary removed seven angels from the angelic hierarchy at a council in Rome in 745 CE. One of these was Uriel. Despite this demotion, the Christian church still recognizes Uriel as Saint Uriel. Even today, Uriel is still celebrated on July 28 by the Egyptian and Ethiopian churches.

This demotion may also be one reason why Uriel is not a popular figure in religious art. However, the most likely explanation is that Uriel was connected with the Johannine heresy that claimed John the Baptist was the true messiah. This was not the case, and Uriel was not involved in any way. However, Pope Clement III (11?–1191) removed a painting of Uriel from the Church of Santa Maria degli Angeli in Rome. Another painting of Uriel, in the Church of Piazza Esedra, was painted over.

As a result of this error, Uriel suffered enormously in Italy, but fortunately his reputation remained intact in the rest of the world. There are many paintings of Uriel in art museums in Spanish-speaking countries, such as Mexico, Argentina, and Colombia.

Dr. John Dee

Francis Barrett, author of *The Magus,* wrote that Uriel brought the great gift of alchemy to mankind.[8] This contribution to civilization is one of the reasons why Uriel is possibly the most invoked archangel of all. It also explains why the great scholar Dr. John Dee was so excited to make contact with him.

In the sixteenth century, Dr. John Dee (1527–1608) was one of the most learned men in Europe. His home in Mortlake, close to London, contained a library of more than three thousand books on the natural sciences. At the time, this library was more complete than those at either Oxford or Cambridge Universities.[9] He was a mathematician, astronomer, philosopher, and the greatest psychic of his day. He was astrologer to Queen Elizabeth I, and after studying her chart, advised her to have her coronation on January 14, 1559. He successfully predicted the approach of the Spanish Armada, and told the queen that Sir Francis Drake's plan of attacking the Spanish ships before they left their home port would probably not be successful. As a result of this, Queen Elizabeth I refused to let Sir Francis Drake act until John Dee said the moment was right.

Dr. Dee also worked extensively with Uriel, and the other archangels. The story of how this happened is a fascinating one.

On December 22, 1581, Dr. Dee and his first scryer, Barnabas Saul, conducted a crystal-gazing session in which

Saul claimed to have seen the Archangel Anael in the ball. John Dee was skeptical, as he considered Anael to be "the Angel or Intelligence now ruling over the whole world."[10] He asked Saul to confirm that this was, in fact, Anael. Another spirit appeared in the ball. John Dee recorded in his diary that this angel was "very beautiful with apparel yellow, glittering, like gold."[11] Even more impressive was his head, which emitted "beams like star beams, blazing, and spreading from it: his eyes fiery."[12] John Dee felt that this was the real Anael. He immediately placed another scrying crystal beside the first, and asked Anael if any angel was assigned to it. Anael told him that Archangel Michael was, but that he would not appear until after Christmas.

This was exciting news, but John Dee was still slightly skeptical because Anael had spelled his name as Annael. However, this matter remained unresolved, as shortly afterwards, Saul was charged with a criminal offense. A few months later, on March 10, 1582, John Dee was introduced to a twenty-six-year-old man who called himself "Edward Talbot." Two days later, Saul, who had been living in John Dee's house, left and never returned.

If Barnabas Saul was a suspicious character, Edward Talbot (1555–94) was even more so. He was lame, and had had at least one of his ears cropped. While working as a municipal scribe in his native Worcester, Talbot had forged a document. In Tudor times, ear cropping was the penalty for forgery.

When Talbot gazed into one of John Dee's crystal balls, he claimed to see Archangel Uriel. This was even more exciting to John Dee than the appearance of Anael, as Uriel was credited with teaching astrology to Enoch.

Thirty years earlier, a French priest had written that one of Enoch's books had been lost to the Europeans but was known to the Ethiopians. It was written in the ancient language that God had taught to Adam. In John Dee's extensive library was a book of lists, tables, and spells called *The Book of Soyga*. John Dee wondered if this was the lost book, and immediately asked Uriel if it was of any value.

"That book was revealed to Adam in paradise by the good angels of God," Uriel replied.[13]

John Dee asked for instructions on how he could read the book. Uriel replied that he could do this, but only Archangel Michael could interpret it. In a second session, later in the day, Uriel gave detailed advice on how the two men could reach Michael. The instructions included reciting certain psalms and praying together.

Uriel then told the men that the house was inhabited by an evil spirit called Lundrumguffa, and that he must be exorcised with brimstone. When John Dee asked when he should do this, Uriel replied, "Tomorrow at the time of prayers."[14]

After they had done this, Talbot said that he saw Uriel dragging the evil spirit away by its legs. He disposed of it by tossing it into a large pit.

"Thus the wicked are scourged," Uriel said.[15] He then left, and reappeared with Michael, who gave him an important message:

> Go forward: God hath blessed thee.
>
> I will be thy Guide.
>
> Thou shalt attain unto thy seeking.
>
> The World begins with thy doings.
>
> Praise God.
>
> The Angels under my power, shall be at thy commandment.
>
> Lo, I will do thus much for thee.
>
> Thou shalt see me: and I will be seen of thee.
>
> And I will direct thy living and conversation.
>
> Those that sought thy life, are vanished away.
>
> Put up thy pen.

At another séance, some days later, Talbot saw Michael with a man whose face was concealed. This man knelt down in front of Michael, who proceeded to dub him with his sword. The man then stood up, and Talbot saw that it was John Dee. Archangel Michael had not only acknowledged John Dee, but had anointed him as well.

After this propitious start, Talbot, who was now known to John Dee by his real name of Edward Kelley, became Dee's full-time scryer.

On April 6, 1583, Uriel appeared again in the ball to announce that John Dee and Edward Kelley had forty days in which to write down the "Book of Secrets." This was the start of a mammoth effort that ultimately produced the secret and sacred language of the angels, known as the Angelic Script, or the Enochian language.

Their method of work was extremely complicated. The angels told John Dee to make a magical table, and a seal of truth, which was a nine-inch wax pentacle, engraved with complex designs. They also had to procure several talismans, a magical ring, a magic mirror, and a new crystal. Edward Kelley sat at the magical table, which contained the crystal and several talismans and pentacles. While he gazed into the crystal, John Dee sat at another table holding a large chart divided into forty-nine by forty-nine squares. Each square contained a letter. Kelley would see an angel in the crystal holding an identical chart. The angel communicated by indicating one letter at a time. Kelley would pass on the column and row number indicated by the angel so that John Dee could find it on his own chart and write it down.

To make it even more complicated, the angels dictated their messages backwards, because the potent energy of the words would otherwise be too powerful to deal with. Despite the slow and tedious method involved, over a seven-year period John Dee and Edward Kelley produced a huge amount of material.[16]

While this was going on, Kelley began seeing visions outside the crystal ball. He saw an ocean with many ships, as well as a tall black man chopping off a woman's head. John Dee asked Uriel for the significance of these visions.

"The one did signify the provision of foreign powers against the welfare of this land, which they shall shortly put into practice," Uriel replied. "The other, the death of the Queen of Scots. It is not long unto it."[17]

Both of these predictions came true. The first was the defeat of the Spanish Armada, which occurred the following year, and the second was the beheading of Mary, Queen of Scots, in 1587.

Just before John Dee's death at the age of eighty-one, Archangel Gabriel appeared to him with a message of good cheer.[18] In the course of his life, John Dee had many contacts with Michael, Gabriel, Raphael, and Uriel.

John Dee possibly saw Archangel Uriel on two occasions. On the first of these, Edward Kelley, John Dee's assistant, saw a cherub in a crystal ball.[19] From his knowledge of the Kabbalah, John Dee was able to identify the cherub as "Uriel, the Angel of Light." Edward Kelley saw the cherub in the ball, but it is not certain if John Dee also saw it. However, as early as 1582, the year that Dee and Kelley met, John Dee had a vision in which a child angel floated outside his window, holding a crystal egg. John Dee recognized this child as Uriel.[20]

Although John Dee and Edward Kelley recorded a wealth of information, they appeared to have had no interest in using it themselves. However, some three centuries later, S. L. MacGregor Mathers, one of the founders of the Hermetic Order of the Golden Dawn, saw its potential, and included parts of Enochian magic in Golden Dawn teachings.

John Dee died in 1608, largely forgotten. Shortly before his death, he locked some of his precious notebooks in a chest, and also buried many in the fields near his home at Mortlake. Fortunately, many of his documents were excavated ten to twenty years after his death by Sir Robert Cotton, an antiquarian. In 1662, a confectioner named Robert Jones heard a rattle in an old chest he owned. When he investigated this, he found a secret drawer containing papers, books, and a small necklace. Unfortunately, his maid used about half of the papers to line her pie tins before anyone noticed what she was doing. When the Great Fire of London broke out in 1666, Mr. Jones's widow, Susannah, found the chest too heavy to move, but she took John Dee's papers with her. In 1672, they were shown to a wealthy lawyer and collector, Elias Ashmole, who immediately recognized their value. These hand-written papers were John Dee's *Liber Mysteriorum,* his book of mysteries. He believed that they contained all the secrets of the universe. If it had not been for Sir Robert Cotton, Robert and Susannah Jones, and Elias Ashmole, almost all of Dr. John Dee's writings would have been lost to posterity.

Uriel and the Kabbalah

An ancient Jewish legend says it was Uriel who gave the Kabbalah to mankind. In the Kabbalah, Uriel is associated with the middle pillar of the Tree of Life, and particularly with Malkuth, the Kingdom. Malkuth is the lowest sephirah and represents the world we live in. Malkuth has San-dalphon as its archangel, and the two angels work in con-junction to ensure the survival and health of the planet. Not surprisingly, Uriel is sometimes referred to as the Great Archangel of the Earth.

Archangel of the Earth

As Archangel of the Earth, Uriel is at his peak in spring and summer. He is the angel in charge of the month of Septem-ber. He is responsible for the ripening of the crops, and for looking after all of nature.[21] Uriel is involved with all four seasons of the year. However, as his direction is north, Uriel's personal season is winter.

Naturally, Uriel is the most earthly of the archangels, and acts as a channel between the earth and the divine. He is in charge of bringing God's plan into the material world. On a personal level, he can help you become aware of your essential spiritual nature. On a more universal level, Uriel is in charge of everything Mother Nature does. Consequently, tidal waves and earthquakes are under his jurisdiction. Uriel frequently manifests himself in storms, especially electrical storms, and many people consider the rainbows that follow these to be an indication of his presence. Not surprisingly, Uriel is associated with Uranus, the planet that is associated with electricity, and sudden flashes of inspira-tion and enlightenment.

Because of his close involvement and intimate connec-tion with the planet, Uriel is also guardian of the nature spirits—the gnomes, sylphs, undines, salamanders, fairies, and sprites who live in the elements of fire, earth, air, and water. These spirits assist nature and keep the world as beautiful as possible.

Uriel is tender yet strong. He brings peace and tranquility to those who need it. He releases pain and trauma from the past. He helps people who are unable to give or receive. He provides the gift of prophecy, as well as insights and inspiration. He encourages creativity, especially in music and literature. He is powerful, organizing, and motivating. He knows your past and your future, and is prepared to help you make the most of every opportunity.

Uriel has been known by a number of names, including Auriel, Hamiel, Hanael, and Phanael. Auriel means "Light of God," Hamiel means "Grace of God," Hanael means "I, the God," and Phanael means the "Face of God." Phanael, or the Face of God, is the source of the familiar, ancient blessing that the Lord gave to Moses: "May the Lord make his face shine upon thee, and be gracious unto thee." (Numbers 6:25)

Uriel also has a number of titles, including Angel of the Eleventh Hour, Angel of Repentance, Angel of Prophecy, Prince of the Sun, Angel of Thunder and Lightning, Angel of Salvation, and Angel of Terror.

This last title shows that, like the other archangels, Uriel is willing to use his power when necessary. He is also known as the Master of Tartarus. In Greek mythology, Tartarus is the purgatory where the wicked were sent to be punished after death. In *Paradise Lost,* iii. 690, John Milton proclaims Uriel as "Regent of the Sun."

A number of colors have been associated with Uriel. Silver and red are the usual choices, but gold, orange, yellow, purple, and pale blue can also be used.

I have left the most important quality of Uriel until last. Uriel is also known as Auriel, the Archangel of Light. This is the divine light that mystics receive when they experience sudden insights that make them as one with God. However, this is not reserved solely for highly evolved, spiritual people. Uriel wants you to receive divine light, and will do everything he can to help you experience it. William G. Gray wrote: "A single flash from Auriel will put us closer to God in an instant than centuries of our muddling speculations."[22]

Transformation

Uriel works in an extremely subtle manner, and frequently you'll discover that he has answered your call by giving you a unique idea that solves your problem. He is known as the Angel of Transformation, as he is able to turn situations completely around and give us a fresh perspective. Uriel helps us understand that something that caused enormous disappointment at the time may later be seen as a wonderful blessing.

Petunia, a former neighbor of mine, had been married for more than twenty-five years and was devastated when her husband was killed in a boating accident. After the funeral, she visited her mother-in-law and met many of her husband's relatives for the first time. One of them worked with stained glass. He taught the basics of the craft, and Petunia returned home with a new hobby that quickly turned into a successful, full-time business. If her husband had not died so tragically, Petunia would never have discovered her ability at stained-glass work. She credits her transformation from grief to happiness through creativity to Uriel.

"Someone was looking after me," she told me. "And I know exactly who it was—Uriel. I talk to him all the time now."

Peace and Tranquility

Archangel Uriel is prepared to help you whenever you need to find inner peace. If you find yourself dwelling on past mistakes or about what might have been, or are full of inner turmoil, call on Uriel for help. Feelings of guilt, negativity, anger, or frustration hold us back from following our true path. We have all been hurt by the actions of others. It makes no difference if the hurt was deliberate or accidental, as the pain is just the same. It is essential that we forgive others, and also forgive ourselves. Of course, forgiveness is not easy. We often want to hold on to our frustration or rage, sometimes even when we know these feelings are harming us more than the other person ever did. Uriel can release us from this self-inflicted burden.

One of my students had been carrying around feelings of guilt for many years. When Brenda was in her early twenties, she had spent a summer in Europe with some college friends. One morning, she woke up with a bad headache, and decided to spend a quiet day in the hostel rather than go sightseeing with her friends. Another girl in the hostel was delighted to take her place in the minibus. A few hours later, the bus was involved in an accident, and the person who had taken Brenda's place was killed. Although Brenda hardly knew this young woman, she felt incredibly guilty. If she had not woken up that morning with a headache, she would have been sitting in that seat, and would have been the one who died. She spent years thinking about the accident, and came to the conclusion that she was virtually a murderer, as her actions had cost the life of someone else. Fortunately, Uriel was able to help her release those painful memories, and give her the peace of mind and soul that she so desperately needed.

Humans are extremely good at creating their own problems. Fortunately, Uriel is always willing to help us in these situations. Nathan, one of my students, made a bad mistake with his girlfriend, who was actively involved with a charitable organization. He thought it would be fun to send her a letter, ostensibly from the organization, praising her for her hard work and effort. When his girlfriend received the letter, she thought it was genuine, and proceeded to tell everyone she knew about it. Word of this got back to the staff at the organization, who sent her a rather curt note saying that although they greatly appreciated her voluntary work, her contribution was neither more nor less valuable than that of anyone else. She was mortified by this, and felt that she had made a fool of herself. Nathan confessed to what he had done, and said that the situation had gotten way out of hand. All he had wanted was for her to feel good. Rather than accepting his confession and apology, she ended the relationship. Nathan did everything he could to see her again, but she refused.

Nathan became depressed as a result. He knew that he had been stupid in forging a letter on the charity's letterhead, but felt that he should be forgiven, as he had done it with good intentions. When Nathan told the class what had happened, one of the other students immediately suggested that he ask Uriel to provide forgiveness.

Nathan replied by saying that he had thought of this, but had not communicated with Uriel, as he felt so guilty about what had happened. However, he agreed to do it. In fact, immediately after the class ended, he went to the top of a nearby hill, and called to Uriel, asking for forgiveness for all his mistakes, and requesting peace and harmony in his life. Immediately, Nathan felt as if a weight had been lifted off his shoulders. The change in him was so profound that when he returned home that night, his mother asked what he had been up to, as he looked happier than he had in months, and all the stress and strain had left his face.

Although, as far as I know, Nathan did not win back his old girlfriend, he was able to find the forgiveness he needed, and is now progressing with his life.

Giving and Receiving

Many people find it hard to give freely, while others give so much that they suffer as a result. Others find it hard to receive anything. These people even find receiving a compliment hard to handle. If you have problems in any of these areas, call on Uriel for help. He will be happy to release these bonds, and set you free.

Anthony had a difficult childhood in a family that was always short of money. Although he had become successful in his business life, Anthony found it incredibly hard to give anything away. This changed when he watched a friend give a beggar several dollars.

"Why did you do that?" he asked. "He'll only spend it on booze or drugs."

"I know," his friend replied. "But it made me feel good."

Anthony was puzzled by this reply, as in his experience, money was something that was earned and never given away. He began watching other people giving money and time to help others. He noticed that they appeared to gain pleasure and satisfaction from their generosity. He experimented himself, but gained no pleasure or satisfaction from it.

This bothered him, and he began asking others about their giving habits. Eventually, someone suggested that he contact Archangel Uriel. Uriel told him that he would never receive any joy from giving until he adopted the practice of giving freely rather than grudgingly. Anthony is now more successful than ever, and is deriving enormous pleasure out of giving to others.

Service to Others

If you feel the need to serve or help others in any way, Uriel is willing to do everything he can to help you. Uriel is interested in the well-being of the planet, and anything that you do to benefit humanity or the world will receive his help and support.

Nanette wanted to help the young people in her community, but was rebuffed everywhere she went. People suspected her motives as she had no family of her own. After being turned down several times, Nanette asked Uriel for help. For some weeks, nothing happened, but then she was offered three opportunities in less than a week. Nanette was able to accept two of them, and is now deriving enormous satisfaction helping young children with learning disabilities in her local area. She has been written up in her local paper, and was described as an "unsung hero."

Prophecy

Uriel is the Archangel of Prophecy and is willing to help you develop your psychic and intuitive skills. He can provide insights through visions, dreams, and sudden perceptions. Once he knows that you are interested in developing these talents, he will provide regular, ongoing assistance.

Norman became interested in the Tarot after having a reading at a psychic fair. He bought a deck of cards and an instruction book, and tried to teach himself. It was more involved than he had thought, and after a few weeks he put the cards away, thinking that they were not for him. Shortly after this, he began having strange dreams. In each of them, he was helping others through his skill at reading cards. After a week of this, Norman began studying the cards again. This time he felt as if someone was looking over his shoulder and guiding him.

"I was amazed when my wife said it must be an angel," he told me. "She thought it might be a guardian angel. We couldn't believe it when we discovered it was Archangel Uriel!"

Norman asked Uriel to guide him with his first readings. Encouraged by the success of these, Norman continued studying the cards and is now working part-time as a Tarot card reader.

"The secret is to involve Uriel," he says. "He'll help you take it as far as you want to go."

Clarity and Insight

Uriel is prepared to help you gain greater insight and clarity about the motivations of others. Once you allow Uriel to help you in this way, you are less likely to be hurt by the hidden agendas or secret ambitions of others.

Claude was a sales representative who was promoted to sales manager of the company he worked for. He was thrilled with the unexpected promotion, but found it hard to be in an office all day after many years spent calling on customers. He also found that he received little support from the people in the office.

After several months of frustration, he called on the angelic kingdom for help, and Uriel replied, giving Claude insight into what was going on in the office. The office staff resented Claude's appointment, as they felt that someone else was more worthy of the promotion. Consequently, they were undermining him in every way they could. Even the one person he trusted was apparently secretly working against him.

With the sudden clarity that this insight gave him, Claude was able to speak to his staff individually, and gradually the problem was resolved. The hardest person to deal with was the one Claude had trusted, and Uriel was able to provide the additional insight Claude needed to handle this delicate situation. This person had coveted the job, and was trying to make Claude's life miserable in the hope that he would leave. Over a period of time, Claude won this person over, and now has a smooth-running department with a happy, hard-working staff.

Prosperity

Uriel wants people to prosper and become successful. Consequently, he is willing to help people who are prepared to work hard and help themselves, to move ahead. If you need more money for any purpose, or simply desire to become more prosperous, ask Uriel for help.

Jacky became upset and worried when she was laid off from her job. She was divorced and was bringing up two children on her own. Her first thought was to find another job. She thought she could find another secretarial job fairly easily. However, she wanted to better herself, and simply replacing one modestly paid job with another would not help that. She asked Uriel for help.

A day later, she decided to open up her own business, offering secretarial services for small businesses. Despite having very limited capital, she was able to lease the necessary equipment, and start work right away. She spent all her spare time calling on potential customers, and soon had all the work she could handle. Today she has three employees, and owns the building from which she operates her business. She credits Uriel with inspiring and motivating her to succeed.

Now that you know something about Uriel, and what he can do for you, it is time to meet him. We will start on this in the next chapter.

Two

HOW TO CONTACT URIEL

URIEL is willing to give you peace and love anytime you need it. Because of this, Uriel is arguably the most accessible of the archangels, bringing harmony and peace of mind to even the most difficult types of situations. Many people have told me how Uriel appeared almost magically when they desperately needed him. It can be comforting to know that he is never far away, and will come to your aid whenever you need him. You may have experienced Uriel's presence in the past without knowing it. Sometimes, while sitting in front of a fire, I feel a sense of peace and tranquility come over me, and realize that Uriel is there with me.

However, there will also be times when you are not in desperate need, but still wish to make contact with Uriel. You might want to thank him for what he has done for you. You might want to gain some understanding about letting go of fear, guilt, or some aspect of the past. You might need his help to forgive someone who has hurt or wronged you. You might want to experience his love around you.

You will find it highly beneficial to establish and maintain a relationship with Uriel. People sometimes tell me that you need to be highly evolved spiritually to even think about communicating with an angel or archangel. This is not the case. I believe that anyone can make a connection to the spiritual realms, if they sincerely want to. All you have to do is temporarily put aside your ego, quieten your mind, and send out a message to the angel you wish to contact. When you become aware of the spiritual presence, speak openly, honestly, sincerely, and humbly, holding nothing back. You can rest assured that your requests will be answered. In return, all you have to do is to strive to lead an honest, upright life, genuinely attempting to make the world, or at least your small part of it, a better place for everyone.

There are many ways to contact Uriel, and we will cover some of the most effective ones here. The first thing you need to do is establish a circle of protection around yourself.

Circle of Protection

Sit or stand in the center of the area you will be working in. If you have a compass with you, or have some idea as to where the four main directions lie, face north. This is because north is Uriel's direction. Take several slow, deep breaths, each time inhaling as much air as possible. Hold the breath for a few seconds before exhaling slowly. Imagine that each breath of air is filling you with protective energy.

After several deep breaths, walk around your chair in a clockwise direction, saying out loud, "Thank you, Uriel, for giving me the opportunity to call on you. I am establishing this circle of protection so that nothing but good can enter." The circle can be as large, or as small, as you wish. You need mark the circle with your steps only once, as this is sufficient to provide all the protection you may need. However, I know many people who like to walk around it several times.

Once the circle has been created, you can do whatever you wish inside it, confident that you are protected and safe. If you know where the four cardinal directions are, you might like to acknowledge and thank the archangels of each direction: Raphael (east), Michael (south), Gabriel (west), and Uriel (north).

You should establish a circle of protection around yourself before working on any of the following exercises.

Meditation

Find a quiet place where you will not be disturbed for at least thirty minutes. You might want to temporarily disconnect the phone, if you are doing this at home. The room should be warm, but not hot. If the weather is cool, you might want to heat the room or cover yourself with a blanket. I like to do this meditation lying on the floor. This is because I tend to fall asleep when doing this exercise in bed. You might prefer to sit in a comfortable chair.

Close your eyes and take several slow, deep breaths. Focus on your breathing, and allow yourself to relax with each exhalation. Gradually allow all the muscles of your body to relax. I usually start with my feet, and then feel the relaxation spreading throughout my body. Once you feel totally relaxed, mentally scan your body and see if there are any areas of tension remaining. Consciously relax these, and then scan yourself again to ensure that you are totally relaxed.

Once you have reached this stage, take another deep breath, and exhale slowly. In your mind, picture yourself sitting in a beautiful garden. It is dusk, and you are watching the night fall, while enjoying the pleasant scent of the beautiful flowers that are all around you. You are pleasantly warm, and feel relaxed and contented. You are aware of a sense of anticipation. You watch the sun slowly disappear over the horizon. Suddenly, it is dark, and you notice a large hand in front of you, palm upwards. It surprises you that you haven't noticed it before, as it is a huge hand. The reason you can see it at all is because there is a flame burning on the palm of this hand. As the hand is held steady, you realize that the hand is experiencing no pain. You know that this is the symbol of Uriel, and that the flame is the fire of love. You gaze at the flame, and watch it flicker and dance. This is Uriel's gift to mankind, a flame of love that can provide you with emotional healing and peace of mind whenever you need it.

As you gaze at the flame, you become aware that the flame is burning in the palm of Uriel's hand. Uriel is there with you, and you can ask him for whatever you desire.

Despite this realization, you do not feel nervous or overwhelmed by the knowledge that you are sitting in a garden with an archangel. In fact, you feel totally relaxed and at peace. You feel more at peace than you have ever been before. You understand that you are surrounded and enfolded by Uriel's love and compassion. Anything you say to him will be listened to and acted upon, because Uriel loves and cares for you. You feel that you can discuss anything that is on your mind, because Uriel will listen sympathetically, and help you gain release and closure.

Spend as long as you need with Uriel. He is patient and will always allow as much time as necessary to help you resolve your problems. When you have finished, thank him sincerely for his love, support, and help. Once you have said goodbye, you will notice the hand and the flame becoming fainter and fainter until they disappear completely. See yourself, in your mind's eye, relaxed in the beautiful garden. When you feel ready, return to the room you are in, become aware of your surroundings, and count to five slowly before opening your eyes.

You are likely to feel exhilarated after spending time with Uriel. You will feel more positive about the future, and have a sense of inner peace. Problems that seemed insurmountable before will now seem easy to overcome, and you will have greater insight into the motivations of others.

Your connection with Uriel will increase every time you perform this meditation. With practice, you will reach a stage where you can sit down, take a few deep breaths, and instantly be in the garden conversing with Uriel. However, this meditation is not intended to be a race, and frequently I take several minutes to reach the garden, purely because the process itself is so peaceful and relaxing.

Appearing Flame Meditation

You will need a straight-backed chair for this exercise. Sit down comfortably, and place your hands in your lap. Rest the back of your right hand on your left palm, and allow your left thumb to relax comfortably on your right fingers.

Close your eyes, take a few deep breaths, and consciously relax your body. When you feel completely relaxed, visualize a flame of love descending in front of you and coming to rest on your right palm. You will feel no pain or heat as this occurs. The sensation you feel will be one of overwhelming love as the special qualities of Uriel's flame infiltrate every cell of your body.

As you gaze into the flame, you will sense Uriel's presence. You will feel completely surrounded by his love and peace. If you are fortunate, you might see a glimpse of him on the far side of the flame. However, seeing him is not as important as having the opportunity to speak with him.

You will probably have thought about the matters you wish to discuss with Uriel ahead of time. Tell him about your concerns and worries, but also tell him about your hopes and dreams. Ask him for any help you may require, and thank him sincerely before you close the meditation.

When your conversation is over, say goodbye to Uriel. Once you have done this, the flame will slowly rise from your palm and ascend out of sight. Take a few slow, deep breaths, and open your eyes.

How to Contact Uriel with Music

Uriel has a deep love of music, and will always be near you when you are totally immersed in your favorite music. Uriel will be close no matter what sort of music you like listening to, be it classical, rock, hip-hop, country, new age, or anything else. Consequently, you can gain an extra benefit by communicating with Uriel while listening to music. Choose some of your best-loved music, and play it quietly while sitting in a comfortable chair. Close your eyes and allow yourself to become totally immersed in the music. If the music is soft and gentle, you will soon find yourself completely relaxed. If the music is more vigorous and up-tempo, you will become partially relaxed and, at the same time, mentally stimulated. Both of these states are good for making contact with Uriel.

Remain focused on the music for as long as you wish. When you are ready, ask Uriel to come closer. You might choose to say this out loud, or you may simply think it. You will notice that the music fades into the background because you are now more interested in communicating with Uriel.

If Uriel does not come into your conscious awareness right away, keep suggesting that he come closer and make himself known to you. Remain confident and positive that he will come. In time, you will realize that he is there with you, and may well have been beside you for some time. You might experience a slight change in the temperature of the room, or perhaps a sense of knowing that he is beside you. He may say something to you. You will either hear what he says, or sense it in your mind.

Once you have made contact, tell Uriel why you are communicating with him at this time. Tell him your hopes and dreams. Ask for advice, comfort, or insight. Spend as much time as you wish communicating with Uriel. When the conversation is over, thank him for his time and insights, say goodbye, and return to the music for a few minutes before getting up.

Contacting Uriel Through Your Creativity

Uriel will always be close to you when you are doing something creative. You do not have to write a sonnet or paint a picture to be creative. Working in the garden and cooking a beautiful meal are both highly creative activities. In fact, every time you think a thought, you are being creative. However, as far as contacting Uriel is concerned, the best time is when you are doing something that completely occupies your mind, and you become lost in the process. You may experience this state while playing the piano, taking a photograph, writing a letter, browsing in a bookstore, or choosing a bottle of wine.

The hardest part of the process is to realize that you are in this state, while it is going on. As soon as you make this discovery, stop what you are doing, close your eyes, and silently ask Uriel to come to you. Most of the time, he will appear instantly, and you will be able to enjoy a conversation with him. With practice, you will find that you no longer need to close your eyes. This makes communication with Uriel easier when you are in a public place, such as a store, park, street, or museum.

Quartz Crystal Method

Uriel likes quartz crystal. Consequently, a good way to contact him is to sit down quietly with a piece of quartz crystal in your hands. Close your eyes and gently fondle the crystal. Take several slow, deep breaths, and then ask Uriel to come to you. Usually, this is all that is required, and you will immediately feel his presence. Some people notice a change in the energies of the crystal, but I usually experience an awareness that Uriel is with me. If he does not come immediately, continue caressing the crystal for a few more minutes, and then ask again. This is a particularly pleasant way of contacting Uriel, and I have never had to do it more than three times to make contact.

Grass Ritual

I like to call this method the "grass ritual," as many years ago, one of my students became extremely excited when I announced that we were going to learn the "grass method" of contacting Uriel. This ritual has nothing to do with marijuana. As you will see in chapter 4, Uriel is the Archangel of the Earth, and this method makes use of that as a means to contact him.

Lie down on your lawn, or any other available piece of grass, and relax. You can lie on your stomach or on your back. Close your eyes, and take several slow, deep breaths until you feel totally calm and peaceful.

Think about the earth, and how it is actually your foundation. Feel the sensation of the grass on any areas of exposed skin. Become aware of any sounds, smells, or sensations that come to you. While relaxing in this way, allow yourself to merge, body, mind, and spirit, into the earth, just as if you were sinking effortlessly into it. When you feel this sense of oneness with the earth, say a silent greeting to Uriel, and wait for a reply. The response is likely to be subtle. A thought may appear in your mind, but you are more likely to experience a feeling of infinite love and security. Uriel, through Mother Earth, is holding you in his comforting arms. Experiment with further communication, if you wish, but focus on the feelings of love and protection Uriel is surrounding you with.

When you feel ready to return to your everyday world, take a slow, deep breath, stretch luxuriously, and open your eyes.

Creating a Ritual

A ritual is a series of actions that produces a required result. The eminent esoteric writer and founder of the Society of the Inner Light, Dion Fortune (1891–1946), wrote: "Ritual is meditation expressed in action."[1] This is a good definition, as performing a ritual allows you to get into the correct state to make contact with the universal forces. For our purposes, a ritual is an effective way of making contact with Uriel.

Mass or Holy Communion is a ritual. Someone who takes the exact same route to work every day has made a ritual out of it. The methods of contacting Uriel that we have already covered are, in effect, rituals, also.

There is no reason why you should not create your own ritual to contact Uriel. You can make it as simple or elaborate as you wish. You can perform it indoors or out. You might choose to enact the ritual on your own, or might prefer to perform it with like-minded friends. You might have special props that you would like to use. All of these things are entirely up to you.

First of all, you need to gather together everything you will need, and then create some sacred space. Choose somewhere where you feel safe and secure. A friend of mine starts her rituals outside the room in which she performs them. When she walks through the doorway, she enters her sacred space. I have a circular rug, and frequently use that as my sacred space. Choose your sacred space carefully, and think about what you would like to do as you enter this area. You might like to dip your fingers into a bowl of water to symbolize a cleansing. You might like to play soft music. You might like to dim the lights. Think about what you will wear. You may choose different colors according to the seasons, or possibly work skyclad (naked). It makes no difference what you do, as long as you feel that it adds to the ritual and makes it more meaningful for you.

You might like to have an altar inside your sacred space. In fact, you could even construct an altar as part of the ritual. On top of this, you can place candles, written requests, and objects to symbolize the four elements. You might choose objects of different colors: red for fire, yellow for air, blue for water, and green for earth. You might use crystals that relate to the elements: opal for fire, topaz for air, aquamarine for water, and quartz for earth. You might even choose Tarot cards to symbolize the four elements: Wands for fire, Swords for air, Cups for water, and Pentacles for earth.

Once you are inside the circle, you might like to honor the archangels of the four directions: Raphael (east), Michael (south), Gabriel (west), and Uriel (north). You might choose to bow to them, or perhaps greet them by saying something along the lines of: "I greet you, Archangel Raphael, mighty

Lord of the East. Please bless this ritual, and empower it for good."

Alternatively, as this is a ritual dedicated to Uriel, you might choose to enter the circle and immediately face north to speak to Uriel. You may also want to sit or stand quietly inside the circle for a minute or two before starting the ritual proper. You might even like to greet the goddesses that relate to the four elements: Hecate (fire), Artemis (air), Aphrodite (water), and Gaia (earth). If you are using candles, you should light these before proceeding to the next stage. The purpose of the first stage is to allow you to relax, and to think about your purpose in conducting the ritual. You might like to raise the energy of your sacred space by beating on a drum, humming, chanting, singing, or breathing rhythmically. Anything that gets you into the right frame of mind is acceptable. One method I find useful is to have a mirror on my altar. I gaze at my reflection in the mirror until I find myself entering an altered state. When this occurs, I know it is time to move on to the next stage.

Finally, it is time to contact Uriel. I like to stand, facing north, with my arms outstretched and my legs wide apart. Most of the time I speak out loud, but if there are people within earshot, I would probably say the words silently. What you say is, of course, entirely up to you. I start the ritual by saying: "Mighty Uriel, Archangel of Peace and Tranquility, please come to my aid. Mighty Uriel, Angel of Ministration, please answer my call. Uriel, Angel of Insight, Love, and Vision, fill me with your peace. Help me let go of the past, so that I can live in the present and serve you to the best of my ability."

Once I have said these words, I wait until I receive a response that tells me that Uriel is with me. Once that occurs, I relax and speak to Uriel about my concerns in exactly the same way I would if discussing them with a close friend.

Once I have discussed everything I need to know with Uriel, I thank him, and then sit quietly for a while to absorb all the information I have received. I might even go into a trance for a minute or two. Certainly, time means absolutely nothing while you are inside your sacred space. The format of your ritual is entirely up to you. I suggest that you practice the format described here, and gradually make changes that feel right for you.

Finally, I thank the archangels of the four directions for their protection and support, and then step out of the circle. A lady I sometimes work with always recites the Lord's Prayer at the end of any ritual. She finds that it effectively closes off the ritual for her, and saying the familiar words out loud is, in effect, a small ritual on its own. The closing off after a ritual is extremely important. You will have opened yourself up inside your sacred space, and you should not return to your everyday life until you have returned to normality.

A good way of doing this is to relax for five or more minutes before carrying on with your day. You might like to have something to eat and drink afterwards, too. As I dislike eating before a ritual, I almost always have something to eat afterwards.

How to Make Instant Contact with Uriel

Most of the time, your contacts with Uriel will not be urgent. However, there may occasionally be situations in which you need to make an instantaneous connection with Uriel. If you are experiencing an emotional turmoil that threatens to get out of control, for instance, you should not hesitate to make immediate contact. All you need do in this type of situation is to call out: "Uriel, I need you now. Please come to my aid." Uriel will respond immediately to any emergency, and will provide calmness and peace of mind, to enable you to better handle the situation.

Sometimes in an emergency situation, you may neglect to thank Uriel afterwards. He will understand, but will appreciate you contacting him later to thank him properly.

Practice, Practice, Practice

Everyone is different. Some people seem to have a natural talent that enables them to contact the angelic realms on their first attempt. They may find it hard to understand people who need to practice for days, weeks, or months before achieving success.

Do not become despondent or give up if you experience difficulty in contacting Uriel. Once you succeed, you will know exactly how to do it again whenever you wish. I recommend that you try to contact him every day for seven days, and then make no further attempts for another week. Then start the process again. Repeat this until you finally make contact. In your sessions, tell Uriel why you wish to contact him. You should also mention that you will be trying to contact him during the next seven days, and would love to hear from him within that time frame. Open up your heart, and allow it to happen when the time is right.

Now that you know how to contact Uriel, it is time to move on to the next stage. In the next chapter we will take a major step forward, and learn how to ask Uriel for assistance.

Three

HOW TO REQUEST ASSISTANCE

DESPITE his reputation, Uriel is gentle, kind, and approachable. He is endlessly patient and helpful. He wants people to better themselves, and to become closer to God. However, he does not like people who have deliberately chosen evil over good. *The Apocalypse of Saint Peter* tells how Uriel punished blasphemers by hanging them by their tongues over a fire that would burn for eternity.

If your motives are for the good of everybody concerned, and you are trying to progress, Uriel will be more than willing to help you. All you need do is tell him openly and honestly everything that is on your mind.

Uriel has many names, because he is associated with a wide range of activities. This means that he can help you in most areas of your life.

Because he is an archangel, many people speak to him in an extremely formal, sometimes even archaic, style. There is no need to do this. Uriel is extremely down-to-earth, and once you have made contact, you can talk to him in the same way you would talk to any close friend.

Uriel is keen to help you, but also wants you to help yourself. He will be more willing to come to your aid if he knows that you have tried to solve the problem on your own, and have called on him for assistance only because you have been unable to resolve it. He is less inclined to help people who won't help themselves.

Another important aspect of communicating with Uriel is to listen. Conversations are not supposed to be one-sided. Tell Uriel your problems and concerns, ask him for help, and then listen for his reply. The response may not come in the way you thought it would. You may hear his reply clearly. You may experience thoughts that clarify or answer your questions. You may not receive an immediate reply, but will finish the conversation reassured and confident that Uriel will help. You may even finish the communication with the feeling that nothing has happened, only to discover later on that the problem has been resolved.

You can communicate with Uriel anywhere. In good weather, I enjoy conversing with him outside in the fresh air. Uriel is the Archangel of the Earth, and it feels appropriate to communicate with him surrounded by nature. Sometimes I do this while walking in the country. At other times, I might find a pleasant place to sit and talk. I have an oracle tree not far from my home, and I enjoy sitting with my back against the trunk of this tree, enjoying a conversation with Uriel.[1]

Some people feel a bit hesitant about talking with an archangel directly. If this is a concern, start by writing letters to Uriel. Your letters should be friendly and chatty, just as if you were writing to a close friend. Express your love and thanks at the end of your message, and then sign your name. Put it in an envelope, and write Uriel's name on the front.

Once you have written the letter, you need to send it to Uriel. You can do this by burning the letter and watching the smoke carry your message to Uriel. Naturally, it is better if you make a small ritual out of doing this. You will need a gold or purple candle. Light this, and sit in front of it, ideally facing north, as that is Uriel's direction. Rest the back of your right hand in the palm of your left, and hold the envelope on your right palm, held in place by your left thumb. Close your eyes and silently tell Uriel that you are sending a message to him. Once you have done this, open your eyes, kiss the envelope, and then hold it in the flame of the candle. Watch the smoke rise heavenwards, and visualize your message reaching Uriel. Once it has been completely burned, thank Uriel sincerely, put out the candle, and carry on with your day. There is no need to even think about your letter again. You have sent it to Uriel, and he will attend to it.

Emotional Healing

This is the area where most people can benefit from Uriel's help. Emotions always overrule logic, and this is why we all sometimes say or do things that we later regret. Tension and stress get stored in the body, usually across the shoulders and in the solar plexus. Until you let go of this negative energy, caused by your emotions, you will be unable to find inner peace and contentment.

Before calling on Uriel, spend as much time as possible observing yourself. Do not make any judgments. Simply watch yourself in all your interactions with others. Make notes afterwards, if you feel it will help. After doing this for a few days, pause and think about your reactions to what is going on in your life. Decide what you are happy with, and what you would like to change. Once you have done this, you will be in a good position to have a serious talk with Uriel about your emotional life.

Start by telling him what you have been doing. Ask him to help you understand why you have been behaving in the way you have. Because you are a product of everything that has happened to you in this lifetime, as well as all your previous incarnations, the underlying cause might lie well back in the past. Uriel will be able to help you recall what happened, and give you advice on how to resolve the situation.

While you are having this discussion, ask him to release all the blockages in your body caused by your emotions. Ask him to help you handle your emotions in a more mature, adult way so that you will stop storing negative emotions in your physical body. Your emotions are an essential part of your makeup, of course, and they play a vital role in developing compassion and intuition. However, many people are totally ruled by their emotions, and cause enormous pain and suffering to themselves, as well as those they come into contact with.

Love

Uriel is often depicted carrying a flame. This is the flame of eternal love. It encompasses the love that we feel for the people who are closest to us, as well as a more detached love towards humanity as a whole. Many people find it hard to give or receive love. They may have been badly hurt in the past, and protect themselves by withdrawing into themselves. They may have given and given in the past, and received nothing in return. This may have made them cynical or cold. Others may have an overly idealistic view about love that condemns them to endless disappointment, as no one can live up to their abnormally high expectations.

Uriel is prepared to help you with any problems or difficulties concerning love. A series of conversations with Uriel on this topic will help you understand that you can have as much love and friendship as anyone else. All you have to do is stop looking for love and friendship for yourself, and give it to others instead, without seeking any reward. When you help others in this way, you will discover that your life has somehow become blessed with love and friendship in abundance.

The Pleasure-Pain Syndrome

We all want to lead happy, successful lives that contain as much pleasure, and as little pain, as possible. Naturally, we revel in every moment of pleasure, and we seek to minimize pain by distracting ourselves with pleasurable activities. However, covering up pain with moments of temporary pleasure is not a permanent solution, and provides only fleeting satisfaction, as the pain continues to fester out of sight. Once you learn to analyze the pain, and look at it dispassionately, you will recognize that the pain is only temporary and there is no need to hang on to it. By doing this, your perception of the situation will change, and you will realize that no matter how difficult a particular situation may be, it will pass in time. Once you realize this, you will cease carrying the pain around with you.

Discuss this when you speak to Uriel. Ask him to help you face pain, and painful situations, without the need of temporary pleasurable distractions. Once you change your way of thinking, and start moving with the flow, accepting both the good and the bad times, you will achieve a state of deep inner peace and joy.

Negative Thinking

My family regularly accuse me of being too positive, as I naturally tend to look on the bright side of life. To use an old analogy, I see the glass as being half-full, while many people see it as being half-empty. However, even though I might be more positive than many people, I still have my share of negative thoughts from time to time. Every day, we think thousands of thoughts, and have no idea how many are positive and how many are negative. If you think more positive thoughts than negative ones, you are likely to be happy and feel in control of your life. Conversely, if you regularly have more negative thoughts than positive ones, you are likely to feel like a victim, and have a gloomy view of your future.

Become aware of any negative thoughts. Each time you do this, deliberately switch the thought around and make it positive. Be alert to anything negative that other people say, also, and refuse to become caught up in it. Other people can be negative if they wish, but you want to remain as positive as possible. I enjoy mixing with positive people, and do my best to avoid anyone who is negative. However, it is impossible to avoid negativity entirely. Watching the news on television is a good example. Be aware that any negativity will have an effect on you.

If you tend to consider the glass to be half-empty, ask Uriel to help you become more positive. Your stress levels will decrease, the ups and downs of life will become easier to handle, and you will feel that you have more control over your life. All of this will have a beneficial effect on your health, worldly success, and spiritual growth.

Guilt

Many people spend their entire lives in a state of guilt. They feel guilty if dinner is not served on time, or they have spent money on themselves. They feel guilty if anything happens to someone in the family, as they should have been able to prevent it. In fact, they feel guilt for existing. If you have a problem with guilt of this sort, Uriel is waiting to help you dissolve it. Obviously, if you are experiencing deserved guilt for something you did, Uriel will not eliminate that. You will have to make amends on your own.

Contact Uriel and explain the situation to him. Tell him about your feelings and how you want to lead a full life, free of guilt. Uriel will listen patiently, and will tell you that you are as worthy as anyone else, and it is right and proper that you nurture yourself. If necessary, he will give you advice on how to stand up for yourself, if the people who have been making you feel guilty continue to put you down. You may need to discuss this matter several times to effect a total cure.

Creativity

Creative people often find it hard to get useful feedback on what they have produced. Their friends and family will naturally say that the work is good, as they do not want to hurt their feelings. Even small groups of like-minded people do not always provide impartial feedback. One lady I know dropped out of a writing group because of the constant negative feedback she received from one of the other members. She later discovered that this person was jealous of her because she had had some short stories published. Fortunately, there is one person you can call on whenever you need help with any kind of creativity.

Uriel is vitally involved in all forms of creativity, and is willing to help you at any stage of the process. If you are looking for a creative idea, call on Uriel for a brainstorming session. You can also call on him if you are stuck at some stage of the project, or are not sure what to do with the final result. In fact, it is a good idea to let Uriel hear or see what you have produced before doing anything else with it. If you have written a poem, for instance, you might want to read it to him. He will give you valuable feedback on what you have produced. If you have completed a sculpture or painting, ask Uriel to look at it and tell you what he thinks.

Of course, you should do this only if you want an honest, impartial assessment of what you have produced. You might be hurt or disappointed with what Uriel has to say. He might dismiss something that you have labored on for a long time. Remember that he knows what you are capable of producing. If he is critical, it means that he believes you can do better.

Consequently, ask him what you should do with the work you have shown him. He might suggest changes you could make. He might suggest that you start again. He might even suggest that you do something completely different. Think about his suggestions, as Uriel wants only the best for you, and will give you genuine, honest feedback. Consult with him while working on your next project. You will be amazed at how quickly you progress when you have Uriel as your creative partner.

Prophecy

Uriel has a special interest in the psychic realms and will be delighted to help you develop your talents in these areas. Not long ago, I spoke to a young woman who had been trying to learn the Runes. She had given it up, as it seemed too hard, and she thought she'd never be able to remember the interpretations for each symbol. I suggested that she try again, but this time do it with the assistance of Uriel. She doubted that it would work, as she thought that an archangel would be far too busy to help a mere beginner. However, she decided to start again, and has made great progress over the last few months. Uriel will do the same for you. All you have to do is ask.

Many people find it hard to analyze their dreams. Dreams normally fade and are forgotten within minutes of getting out of bed. Consequently, it is a good idea to write down everything you can remember as soon after waking as possible. Then, when you are ready, you can enjoy a session with Uriel and ask him about anything you do not understand. Many dreams are prophetic in nature, and Uriel can help you develop this skill so that you will be able to decipher the hidden meanings in your dreams, and also those of others.

Another way in which Uriel can help you develop your prophetic ability is to visit the future in the form of a guided visualization. Sit down quietly and relax. Ask Uriel to join you. When he arrives, tell him that you are interested in having a glimpse into your future, and would like to see what your life will be like three months ahead. Naturally, you can request any time period you wish. You will immediately find yourself, with Uriel's help, visualizing a scene that has yet to take place in the future. Examine it in as much depth as possible, and then return to the present. You might want to ask Uriel about the experience afterwards. When you are ready, thank him and return to your everyday life. With practice, you will be able to experience several different time periods in the one exercise.

The future can be changed. If you are unhappy with anything that you see in your future, you have the power to make changes in the present that will alter the course of your future. Naturally, you should discuss the situation with Uriel before making changes, and then make another visit into the future once you have made them, to see what differences they will make.

Prosperity

Uriel wants you to enjoy a life of happiness and abundance. Prosperity gives you the freedom to make choices in your life, and to do the things that you want to do. Prosperity is more than money in the bank. It is a feeling of abundance and well-being, and affects every aspect of your life. When you live your life with an attitude of abundance, you feel as if you can do and achieve anything.

If you do not have the degree of abundance that you desire, ask Uriel for assistance. He will be willing to help you find ideas that you can utilize to achieve prosperity and abundance in your life.

One of Uriel's main tasks is his responsibility for the planet. Each of the four main archangels is in charge of an element. Michael is in charge of the fire element, Gabriel looks after water, Raphael has air, and Uriel has earth. We will learn how to contact him in his role of Archangel of the Earth in the next chapter.

Four

ARCHANGEL OF THE EARTH, PART ONE

THE cross has been a symbol of Christianity for almost two thousand years. However, it predates Christianity by thousands of years, as it has always been considered a symbol of the cosmos: two intersecting lines that indicate the four cardinal directions. Sometimes, people are symbolically placed in the center. In Babylonian times, it also indicated the four phases of the moon. In Syria, it represented the four great gods of the elements. In China, people believed that tigers guarded the four corners.

Christian missionaries were puzzled at the veneration that primitive people around the world showed to the cross. In Africa, the cross was a sign of protection, while in Scandinavia, it signified fertility. In Central America, the cross symbolized the four rain-bearing winds. The Egyptian ankh, a symbol of immortality, was adopted by the Coptic Church and was transformed into the Christian cross.

The cross also symbolized the Tree of Life. The vertical axis represented ascension, while the horizontal axis indicated life on earth. The vertical axis indicated the heavens, but also the underworld. The horizontal axis indicated the past (left-hand side), present (where the two lines cross), and future (right-hand side).

In the second century CE, Irenaeus, Bishop of Lyon, wrote about the four quarters of the earth indicated by the cross:[1]

> The Gospels could not be either greater or lesser in number than they are. For since there are four regions of the world in which we live, and four Universal Spirits, and since the Church is disseminated over the whole earth, and the pillar and firmament of the Church is the Gospel and the Spirit of Life, it follows that she should have four pillars breathing forth incorruptibility in all directions and vivifying people everywhere.

This is an interesting way of explaining why there should be no more than four gospels, while at the same time effectively dismissing the large number of apocryphal gospels. However, the most intriguing part of what Irenaeus said is his mention of "four Universal Spirits." These are most likely to be the four archangels: Michael, Gabriel, Raphael, and Uriel.

Raphael is in the east, and looks after spring and the element of air. Michael is in the south, and looks after summer and the element of fire. Gabriel is in the west, and looks after fall and the element of water. Uriel is in the north, and looks after winter and the element of earth.

Gradually, more and more attributes became associated with each direction, and a fourfold symbolic system developed. Historians think that the Greek philosopher Empedocles (c. 490–430 BCE) was the first person to teach the concept of the four elements as a complete system. He also introduced the four elements to astrology.

Here are some of the main associations of each element:

Fire

Active

Masculine

Divine energy

Purification

Regeneration

Courage

Sexual power

Gemstone: Fire opal

Age: Youth

Color: Red

Temperament: Choleric

Elemental: Salamanders

Direction: South

Season: Summer

Archangel: Michael

Astrological signs: Aries, Leo, Sagittarius

Air

Active

Masculine

Spirituality

Freedom

Intellect

Impulse

Gemstone: Topaz

Age: Birth

Color: Yellow

Temperament: Sanguine

Elemental: Sylphs

Direction: East

Season: Spring

Archangel: Raphael

Astrological signs: Gemini, Libra, Aquarius

Water

Passive

Feminine

Purity

Cleansing

Emotional

Fertility

Sensuality

Intuition

Purification

Spiritual nourishment

Gemstone: Aquamarine

Age: Middle age

Color: Blue

Temperament: Phlegmatic

Elemental: Undines

Direction: West

Season: Fall

Archangel: Gabriel

Astrological signs: Cancer, Scorpio, Pisces

Earth

Passive

Feminine

Nurturing

Protective

Solidity

Steadfastness

Growth

Practicality

Gemstone: Quartz

Age: Old age, death

Color: Green

Temperament: Melancholic

Elemental: Gnomes

Direction: North

Season: Winter

Archangel: Uriel

Astrological signs: Taurus, Virgo, Capricorn

Uriel is the Archangel of the Earth. This is an incredible responsibility, as it involves the mountains, valleys, seashores, lakes, forests, farmlands, caves, towns, and cities, as well as the oceans and climate. Uriel ensures the fertility of the earth, and is responsible for everything the earth provides, ranging from minerals and oil to fruit and flowers. All the blessings that Mother Earth provides, even life itself, are under the direct control of Uriel. Remember that we are formed from earth, and our physical bodies return there once this incarnation is over. Earth also provides us with the food, shelter, and clothing we need to survive.

You can experience the magic of the earth in many different ways. It occurs whenever you walk barefoot along a beach or on a grassy meadow. On these occasions, if you pause for a few moments, you can feel the magic of the earth entering you and rejuvenating every cell of your body. Have you ever sat entranced by a magnificent view? Or gazed in admiration at the perfect form of a leaf or a flower? Or held a crystal in your hand? Or heard a gurgling brook? Or listened to the song of a bird? Or opened a window and seen the morning dew? Uriel is close to you whenever you do any of these things.

Uriel is actively involved in all earthly matters. He loves gardeners and people who work intimately with nature. However, he is also vitally interested in any earthly goal. Consequently, business, real estate, construction, investments, the stock market, money, and careers all come into his areas of interest.

Uriel's interests can even be taken a step further. Various qualities, such as determination, industry, ambition, concentration, responsibility, and strength of character, can all be related to the earth element, and consequently to him. You can ask Uriel for help if you wish to develop these character traits.

You can harness the element of earth to help you achieve your goals. Obviously, you should do this mainly for material, or earthly, goals. However, you can also use the earth element for any goal or request that needs Uriel's assistance.

Grounding

It is important to learn how to ground yourself in the earth whenever necessary. You need grounding whenever you feel restless, confused, agitated, or unable to concentrate. You may also need grounding if you have been doing something energetic, or have built up excess energy. The most important time to pause and ground yourself is when you are overcome with a strong emotion, such as anger. Many of the reports of violence you read about in the newspapers would not have occurred if the people involved had learned how to ground themselves.

Fortunately, there are a number of simple ways to quickly ground yourself. The easiest method is to place your hands firmly on the ground for several seconds. Another method is to visualize yourself growing roots deep down into the ground. Yet another method is to hug, or hold on to, a tree. Any wood that is in contact with the earth will do, if there are no trees around. People tend to scoff at "tree-huggers," but they are probably saner and definitely more grounded than the people who laugh at them. I will have more to say about tree-huggers in the section on trees.

Experiment with grounding yourself at different times during the day. Touch, hold, or even hug a tree, and see what it feels like. If you are feeling upset or angry, you are likely to experience a rapid sense of release, followed by sensations of peace. If you are feeling happy and contented, you will experience Uriel's energy coming into every cell of your body from the tree. You will experience benefit, no matter what mood you happen to be in.

Sand

Sand is a wonderful element that is often under-utilized by people working with the earth energies. Because it consists of countless tiny grains, sand has always been considered a symbol of infinity. In arid regions, where there is a lack of water, sand is used for cleansing. Consequently, it is also associated with purification.

Sand is particularly useful when working with the Archangel of the Earth. It can be scattered over a wide area, carried in a pouch, or placed in a bowl, depending on your particular needs.

You can buy sand, or you can collect your own from a beach, river, or desert. If you gather your own sand, make sure that you leave the beach or riverbank in a better condition than when you arrived. Pick up some litter and say a prayer of thanks.

Let's assume that you are suffering from stress and are seeking Uriel's help to grant you peace and tranquility. Pick up a handful of sand in your dominant hand. Close your fingers over it, and rest the back of this hand in the palm of your other hand. Face north, which, as you know, is Uriel's direction.

Close your eyes and focus on your desire for peace and tranquility. Think about the changes that will take place in your life once you are free of whatever it is that has been causing the stress.

Spend as long as you wish thinking about these things. When you feel ready, ask Uriel to help you achieve your goal. Speak to him, either silently or out loud, telling him exactly what you want, and why you desire it. Finally, ask him for his help and blessing. Wait for a response. As you know, this can come in a variety of forms, but you will sense it immediately when it is given. Once you have Uriel's blessing, thank him sincerely. Pause for a few moments, and think once more about your goal, and how Uriel will help you achieve it.

Open your eyes, and feel the sand in your hand. What you do now depends entirely on you. The handful of sand is now imbued with Uriel's energy. If you are living in a highly stressful environment, you might want to encircle your home with grains of sand. Alternatively, you might choose a quiet place and scatter the sand in all four directions. You might decide to sprinkle a little in different rooms in your home or workplace. You might place some in a bowl or container. You might want to place some in a pouch or bag that you can carry with you. You can do all of these things, if you wish.

Salt

In the Sermon on the Mount, Jesus described his disciples as "the salt of the earth" (Matthew 5:13). This illustrates the value and importance that salt has always possessed. Salt also symbolizes morality, spirituality, hospitality, and friendship. Because salt is incorruptible, it was used as an offering in Hebrew sacrifices. The ancient Greeks and Romans considered salt to be protective. It preserved food, and therefore could probably protect people. Salt was also considered a symbol of immortality, as the ancients discovered that its basic properties do not change when mixed with other elements.

Salt was extremely valuable, as it was difficult to mine. In ancient Rome, soldiers were sometimes paid in salt. This is the derivation of the word *salary*, and the expression "not worth his salt." In ancient Greece, people would be welcomed with an offering of a few grains of salt in their right hand. This ensured that the visitor would be safe in the host's home.

Salt is a useful tool that absorbs negative energy. It can be used to help you release tensions, anxieties, fears, and negativity. You can easily demonstrate this to yourself. All you need do is fill a bath with warm water, pour in some bath salts, and relax in the water for a while. By the time you get out, your problems will have diminished considerably.

Ordinary household salt can be used to eliminate negativity anywhere. You can sprinkle some outside all the entrances to your home to capture any negative energy before it comes indoors. An acquaintance of mine also sprinkles salt on all the windowsills of her home. In Japan, salt was frequently used for protection. Even today, some people in Japan sprinkle salt inside their homes to remove negative energies after an unpleasant or disagreeable person has left.[2]

In Europe, people used to carry a small quantity of salt with them to ensure success in everything they did. The salt also acted as a protection at night. You can carry a few grains of salt in your pocket or purse to eliminate any negativity that you encounter in your everyday life.

An old superstition says that it is bad luck to spill salt. In Leonardo da Vinci's painting *The Last Supper,* Judas Iscariot has spilled the salt. This is just one example of the symbolism in this painting. A pinch of salt thrown over the left shoulder traditionally averts bad luck. Good spirits were supposed to live on the right side, while negative spirits lived on the left. Consequently, when you tossed salt over your left shoulder, there was a possibility of hitting demons in the eye.

Trees

Trees have been associated with magic since before recorded history. Because they have roots buried deep within the earth and branches that reach up to the heavens, they are symbols of power, longevity, and spiritual growth.

It has become fashionable to deride tree-huggers. My children are all adults now, but they still disappear quickly if they think I'm about to hug a tree. Apparently, it's not cool to be seen with a tree-hugger. All the same, trees are willing to provide anyone with energy, at any time. All you need do is choose a suitable tree and give it a good hug. Hugging trees is also an effective way of curing a headache or warding off a cold.

I discovered the amazing power of trees when I was a child. There was a row of oak trees beside the sports field at the school I attended. I found it enormously energizing to stand with my back against the trunk of an oak tree, and to hug the tree behind my back. I was able to follow what was happening in the game, and at the same time reap the benefits of this intimate contact with a tree.

I usually prefer to face the tree while hugging it. However, that would have been impossible at high school, where I was considered strange enough anyway. If you have never hugged a tree before, here are some suggestions to make the experience as beneficial as possible.

Find a tree well away from other people. You do not want to be disturbed. Take off your shoes and socks and stand several feet away from the tree. Roll your shoulders and then consciously relax your body. Feel the weight of your body in the soles of your feet. Slowly walk towards the tree, feeling the earth beneath your feet. Walk right up to the tree, and look up into the branches. Slowly lower your eyes until you are looking at the ground. Think of the roots of this powerful tree doing their work beneath the ground.

Think about your feet, and feel the earth's energies rising up and flowing through your body. You will feel your heart opening up. When this happens, hug the tree with both arms. The healing energy of the tree will restore, invigorate, empower, and stimulate you. In fact, you are likely to feel overwhelmed by the sensations you experience when you first experiment with this.

Hugging trees is also a good way to contact Uriel. All you need do is find a suitable tree, hug it, and ask for Uriel. You will feel his presence almost as soon as you have asked for him. Tell him what you want, and leave it in his hands. Some people scratch their request in the earth in front of the tree before hugging it. I sometimes draw something to symbolize what I want, but most of the time I prefer to discuss the matter directly with Uriel.

Herbs and Flowers

The plant kingdom is essential for human life. Plants and trees absorb carbon dioxide, and give us life-essential oxygen. This shows how everything on this planet is interconnected, and how we need to maintain the balance of nature.

Flowers and herbs symbolize spirituality, beauty, and the brevity of life. Herbs also symbolize modesty and hidden talents. The cuplike shape of flowers, along with their different colors and perfumes, symbolize femininity. White flowers symbolize innocence but also death, while yellow flowers are related to the sun. Red flowers symbolize blood and life, and blue represent dreams, mystery, and the occult. Violet and gold flowers both symbolize spirituality. In the East, all flowers symbolize the gradual unfolding and awakening of spirituality. Brahma and Buddha are depicted emerging from flowers, and the Virgin Mary is often shown holding a lily.

It is always a pleasure to give, and to receive, gifts of flowers. The ancient Egyptians believed that doing this provided good fortune to both the giver and the recipient. It also honors Uriel to give a gift of his bounty to a friend or relative.

Random Rituals

Whether or not we realize it, we all make regular use of ritual in our lives. Many couples enjoy a drink together before eating their evening meal. That could be described as a ritual. If unexpected visitors arrive, you probably offer them tea or coffee. Preparing the refreshments, and enjoying the results, is a ritual. I walk in the countryside almost every day. I generally pause in a particular place, and enjoy the view for a minute or two before moving on. That has become a regular part of my walk, and could be considered a small ritual.

Churches make regular use of ritual to mark the important phases of life. There are rituals associated with baptism, confirmation (coming of age), weddings, and funerals. The Christian churches realize how necessary ritual is to add meaning to our lives.

You can create earth rituals dedicated to Uriel whenever you wish. There is something powerful and magical about creating rituals outdoors. The energy varies, depending on the weather, the season, and the time of day. I have performed rituals on cloudless, sunny days, as well as in torrential rain. I have performed them on a crowded beach, and in the middle of a desert. I have conducted rituals at noon and at three AM. You should always expect the unexpected. I once performed a ritual before a flock of ducks, who congregated and watched my every move with great interest. On many occasions, the weather changed dramatically while I was performing the ritual. Sometimes, a visitor or two has strayed into the private spot I had carefully chosen. All of these variables add to the occasion, and most of the time they enhance the experience.

Several months ago, I came across a woman performing a ritual on a secluded beach. I would have loved to have stayed and watched what she did. Obviously, I did not do that. She wanted privacy, and I gave her a wide berth. Please do the same if you ever come across someone performing a ritual of any sort.

I frequently create circles of sacred space out of sand, stones, shells, pine cones, or anything else that is at hand. They satisfy a need in me to honor Uriel, and the energies of the earth. Usually, I leave my circles behind, and enjoy wondering what passers-by will think when they come across them. I also enjoy making sand circles when the tide is out. As the tide comes in again, my circle gradually disappears until the sand is smooth again. This marks the end of my ritual.

Random rituals of this sort still need some sort of structure.

1. The first stage is purification. If I have planned a particular ritual, perhaps to celebrate a solstice, I will bathe beforehand. However, random rituals are not usually planned ahead of time, and consequently the purification stage consists of clearing out all the clutter from my mind so that I can focus exclusively on the ritual. If I am performing the ritual to ask Uriel's help for any purpose, I will think about that, and mentally compose my petition, so that I will not need to pause in the middle of the ritual itself.

2. The second stage is to cast the circle. As I have mentioned, I usually create a circle out of any items that are close at hand. However, this is not mandatory, and you can imagine an area of sacred space, if you wish. I enjoy physically constructing a circle. The physical activity of gathering the necessary

items and forming them into a circle is pleasant, and also gives me more time to think about the ritual. Long ago I learned that it is important not to harbor any negative feelings when I step inside the circle. If I feel angry or agitated, for any reason, I pick up a small object, such as a stone or clump of earth. I hold it between the palms of my hands and mentally transfer all the negativity into it. Once I have done this, I toss it over my left shoulder, well away from the circle.

3. The third stage is to step inside the circle, and bow in all four directions. I like to raise the energy at this stage. I do this by singing, humming, clapping, playing a musical instrument, or dancing inside the circle. In addition to raising energy, these are all right-brain activities, which help me let go of the stresses and strains of everyday life.

4. Frequently, I will take a small object, such as a stone, into the circle with me. This is to symbolically thank Uriel, and I leave it in the center of the circle when I leave.

5. The next stage is the fulfillment of my purpose in having the ritual. In this case, it is to contact Uriel, and this can be done using any of the methods discussed earlier. I welcome Uriel, and then discuss whatever it is I am concerned about.

6. The fifth stage is the completion. I thank Uriel for his help and advice, and say goodbye. I bow in all four directions once more, and finally step outside the circle.

Use your imagination when performing a random ritual. You should be relaxed, open, receptive, and welcoming. Feel free to dance, jump, laugh, cry, sing, or yell. It is your ritual, and you can make it as light or as serious as you wish.

I have described this ritual in the way I do it when on my own. However, you can use as many people as you wish. A group of people, all working with the same aim in mind, can raise enormous power. In practice, virtually all of my random rituals are performed when I am on my own. However, I am a member of a small group of people who work together when performing organized rituals.

Timing

You can communicate with Uriel whenever you need him. However, there are also traditional times that are believed to be better than others for magical purposes. For example, it is usually considered better to make any requests concerning new beginnings, growth, or fertility when the moon is waxing, or at the time of the new moon. Any requests that deal with endings, or overcoming obstacles, should be made at the time of the waning or full moon.

There are many special magic days in the Western magical tradition. Most of these days have been celebrated for thousands of years, and were originally used to mark the solstices, or to celebrate events such as planting or harvesting. Eight of these days are the *sabbats,* which are festivals that mark the changing seasons. These are the summer and winter solstices, the spring and fall equinoxes, and the four fire festivals that occur on the quarter days: Samhain, Imbolc, Beltane, and Lughnasadh. These days all mark the ebb and flow of cosmic energies as we pass through an entire year. You can use all of these days to establish an even closer connection with Uriel.

- January 1 (New Year's Day). New Year's Day has been celebrated for more than five thousand years, but it wasn't until after 153 BCE that the new year officially began on January 1.[3] Even then, there were many disagreements about this, and the date was changed many times until the Gregorian calendar (1582) restored January 1 as the start of the new year. (Incidentally, Dr. John Dee worked extremely hard to introduce this calendar to Britain in 1583. However, Edmund Grindal, the Archbishop of Canterbury, considered the matter Papist, and effectively blocked it. This decision kept Britain out of the Gregorian system for one hundred seventy-five years.) New Year's Day is a good time to make plans for the coming year. You should consult Uriel for help in any areas that seem insurmountable. This is also a good time to discuss financial matters with him.

- January 20 (Transfiguration or St. Agnes' Eve). Christ's transfiguration took place on Mount Tabor (Matthew 17:1–9). Jesus took Peter, James, and John with him up the mountain. They heard the voice of God saying, "This is my beloved Son, in whom I am well pleased." On a cosmic level, this day combines the physical and spiritual worlds, allowing mutual contact. This is a good day for any form of divination. You can speak with Uriel and ask for help in developing your prophetic gifts.

- February 2 (Imbolc or Candlemas). Imbolc is a Gaelic word that means "ewe's milk." It is the sabbat that marks the commencement of lactation in cows and sheep. It is a sign that winter is coming to an end, and spring is not far away. It is a time of rebirth, and is a good time to contact Uriel concerning new starts, such as in work and friendships.

- March 21 (Ostara or the spring equinox). Ostara, or Eostre, was an ancient goddess of fertility. She was associated with eggs and hares, which explains their association with Easter. This is a time of new birth, and the sudden reappearance of colorful flowers, such as tulips and daffodils, symbolizes this. It is a time to set goals, and make specific plans to achieve them. This is a good time to contact Uriel on any matters concerning growth and future development. You should also talk to Uriel about any form of creativity that will take time to complete.

- April 24 (St. Mark's Eve). This is a good evening to call on Uriel for divination purposes.

- April 30 (Walpurgis Night) and May 1 (Beltane). This evening, and the following day, marks one of the most important sabbats in Wicca.

- May 1 (Beltane). This was an important druid festival. It marks the start of summer, and it is believed that as the veil between the physical and spiritual worlds is almost invisible at this time, it is a good time to communicate with angels and other spiritual beings. This is a good time to talk to Uriel about love, family life, and anything that troubles you. It is also a good time to find inner peace.

- June 23 (Midsummer's Eve). The summer solstice is a good time for communicating with any member of the angelic kingdom. It is believed that if you desire dreams that will give insight into the future, you should sleep with mistletoe under your pillow on Midsummer's Eve. This is a carefree time, celebrating the longest day of the year. However, the feelings of joy and fulfillment are tempered by the knowledge that the days will now start to get shorter. This is a good time to speak to Uriel about clarity, vision, and prophecy.

- July 25 (St. James' Day). This is good day for walking outdoors, gathering herbs, and communing with Uriel about spiritual matters. It is a time in which you can get to know him better. Rather than asking him for help with a specific problem (although you can, if necessary), this is a time to thank him for his love and support.

- August 1 (Lughnasadh or Lammas). Lughnasadh is a harvest festival that celebrates the fertility and generosity of the earth. It is a time of thanksgiving. Consequently, this is a good time to thank Uriel for everything he does for you. It is also a time to ask for peace of mind and spiritual growth.

- August 21 (Mabon or the autumn equinox). The days and nights are equal now, creating a brief period of equilibrium. Mabon is a second harvest festival, again giving thanks for the beneficence of the earth. It is a time to communicate with Uriel about close relationships, and to put all matters that are out of your control into his hands.

- October 31 (Samhain or Halloween). This is the death festival, marking the start of winter. It is a time of introspection and transformation. It is a good time to contact Uriel on matters concerning peace, tranquility, repentance, and service to others.

- December 21 (Yule or St. Thomas' Day). This is the winter solstice, which celebrates the return of the waxing sun. It is the time of the longest night, but it also indicates the promise of better times ahead.

It is the Christmas season, and since the nineteenth century people have decorated fir trees at this time. This tree has an interesting history, as at the Roman festival of Saturnalia, evergreen decorations were used to celebrate the end of the old year, and the start of the new. Centuries later, in the pagan "raw nights" (December 25 to January 6), people hung up green branches in their homes to protect themselves from evil spirits.

People also eat too much at Christmas, and this surfeit of food symbolizes abundance. The holly and mistletoe produce berries at this time, symbolizing fertility. This is a good time to contact Uriel on matters concerning growth, creativity, and future plans.

The *esbats* are also excellent times to communicate with Uriel. These are the nights of the full moon, when celebratory rituals are performed. Although the derivation of this word is obscure, some people think it is derived from the medieval French word *s'esbattre*, which means "to celebrate joyfully." The esbats are good times to discuss creative projects with Uriel.

You may have noticed that we have not yet mentioned crystals, one of the most important of the earth elements. We will look at them in the next chapter.

Five

ARCHANGEL OF THE EARTH, PART TWO

STONES, and crystals in particular, have been used for esoteric purposes for thousands of years. Stone Age people were making primitive tools from stones 2,500,000 years ago.[1] So-called primitive people also erected huge stone circles, such as Stonehenge. A fascinating research program, called the Dragon Project, tested some of the standing stones in England and found that they produced a vibrational frequency pattern that could almost be described as singing. They also contain a large percentage of quartz crystal in their composition, which means they are huge energy-conductors.

The fact that crystals can aid meditation, amplify thought energy, manifest light, store energy, and facilitate contact with Uriel has always been known. In addition to this, of course, crystals are incredibly beautiful, and people enjoy working with them.

Crystals come from the earth. Consequently, they are closely associated with Uriel, and can be used in many ways to keep him close to you. Crystals can also be used to contact any other member of the angelic kingdom. Crystals keep us grounded and well-balanced. We need to keep in touch with all four elements to feel complete and whole. I became aware of this when visiting a friend of mine who lives on the twentieth floor of an apartment building. She enjoys an incredible view from her windows, but says she only feels truly centered and balanced when she is on ground level. Not surprisingly, she walks in a local park every day of the year to absorb as much earth energy as possible.

Archangel Crystals

All of the archangels have specific crystals that relate to them. These are usually assigned to them on the basis of color. However, there are also three crystals that can be used to contact any member of the angelic hierarchy. These are celestite, selenite, and rutilated quartz.

Celestite is a light blue stone that is sometimes called angelite. Traditionally, it has been used to remove stress and tension. It also provides harmony and compassion for all living things. It slows down the conscious mind and allows you to connect with the universal forces. It encourages spiritual growth and angelic contact. It enables you to open up and gain inner guidance, frequently through dreams. It is often used by astral travelers and by people wanting to make contact with their spirit guides.

Selenite is a translucent, white crystal that is considered to be one of the most powerful healing stones. In fact, some authorities feel that only qualified therapists should be allowed to use it for healing purposes.[2] Selenite helps balance the emotions, and allows people to let go of painful memories from the past. It also soothes the cares and stresses of everyday life. It is useful in recalling past lives and is also used for psychic protection.

Quartz is a compound of silica and oxygen, and is one of the most commonly found minerals in the world. It has been revered by almost every culture. Large quartz crystals were found in the Egyptian Temple of Hathor, which dates back to 6000 BCE. In the fifth century BCE, the Greek priest Onomacritis said: "Who so goes into the temple with this [quartz] in his hand may be quite sure of having his prayer granted, as the gods cannot withstand its power."[3]

Apollonius of Tyana (c. 3–97), the Greek philosopher, mystic, and seer, used quartz for teleportation purposes. Apparently, he demonstrated this by dematerializing and materializing again in front of Emperor Titus Domitian (51–96). He then dematerialized again and reappeared at the foot of Mount Vesuvius.[4]

Throughout history, people have believed that colorless crystalline quartz enhances visions and clairvoyance. It enables people to "hear" or receive information that they could not obtain in any other way. In the days of crystal set radios, which I am old enough to remember, this aspect of quartz was extended further, when people discovered that quartz allowed them to hear radio transmissions.

All quartz is useful when contacting the angelic realms, but rutilated quartz is considered the most beneficial as it appears to contain angel hair. In actuality, these are fine red, gold, or silver needles of rutile (titanium dioxide) that are encased inside the clear quartz. Traditionally, rutilated quartz has been associated with longevity. It also strengthens the immune system and promotes feelings of well-being and positivity. It enhances spirituality, and provides feelings of peace and contentment. Some people have told me that they thought that the rutile inside the quartz diminished the power of the crystal. In fact, the opposite is the case, and the rutile adds considerable power and energy to the crystal.

Uriel's Crystals

There are many crystals that relate to Uriel, as he responds readily to gold, purple, silver, indigo, blue, orange, and red. Consequently, crystals of these colors are the most suitable ones to use. However, this is still a matter of personal choice. As you know, Uriel is the archangel of the earth element. Consequently, any crystal can be used, as long as you enjoy working with it. Here are some possibilities for you to consider.

Amethyst

The ancient Hebrews believed that the amethyst helped control virtue by stimulating suitable visions or dreams. In Roman times, women felt that wearing an amethyst enabled them to retain the affections of their spouse. Their husbands also wore it as an amulet to protect them in battle. Bishops wear amethyst rings as the purple color is connected with the wine that is transfigured to Christ's blood during Mass. The color purple is traditionally associated with a deep, long-lasting, true love. Amethyst is believed to make negative thoughts positive, and to increase intuition. It also grants serenity, composure, and peace of mind to anyone who wears or carries it.

Ametrine

Ametrine is not an easy crystal to find. It is gold and purple in color, and is used to eliminate phobias and to provide emotional balance. It brings peace of mind, and an acceptance of what has occurred in the past.

Aquamarine

Aquamarine is a blue-green beryl. In Roman times, it was considered to cure damage to the eyes. It was also worn to deepen the bonds of love between two people. Beryl was one of the twelve precious stones that St. John the Divine considered to be the foundation stones of the New Jerusalem (Revelation 21:20). In the tenth century, Andreas, Bishop of Caesarea, connected this stone to the apostle Thomas.

In the Middle Ages, it became popular for divination purposes, and was called the "oracle crystal." One method involved using a bowl of water with the letters of the alphabet arranged around the rim. The crystal was suspended from a thread, creating a pendulum. The thread was held so that the crystal barely touched the water's surface, and moved to spell out the answers to questions that the diviner asked. Another method involved dropping the crystal into a bowl of water and "seeing" answers to questions in the disturbed water. This was usually used to find lost or stolen objects.[5]

Traditionally, aquamarine is a symbol of truth, integrity, and honor. Dreaming of it was also positive, as it signified a rise to a position of high honor. It has always been considered protective, especially of people traveling over water.

Bloodstone

Bloodstone is a dark green stone, containing many inclusions of red and brown iron spots that give it its name. At one time it was commonly known as "bloody jasper." The unknown author of the Leyden papyrus was obviously highly impressed with the qualities of bloodstone, and recommended that it be used as an amulet: "The world has no greater thing; if any one have this with him he will be given whatever he asks for; it also assuages the wrath of kings and despots, and whatever the wearer says will be believed."[6]

Bloodstone was also believed to stop hemorrhaging, and was often used to stop nosebleeds. Interestingly, early

Spanish visitors to the New World found native Americans were using it for the same purpose. Bernardino de Sahagun, a Franciscan friar, wrote in his *Booke of Thinges That Are Brought from the West Indies* (1574):[7]

> The stone must be wet in cold water, and the sick man must take him in his right hand, and from time to time wet him in cold water. In this sort the Indians do use them. And as touching the Indians, they have it for certain, that touching the same stone in some part where the blood runneth, that it doth restrain, and in this they have great trust, for that the effect hath been seen.

An interesting legend tells how the bloodstone was originally a green jasper that was at the foot of Christ's cross. Drops from the Savior's wounds splattered on the stone, and ever since, all bloodstones have carried the evidence of the crucifixion. Because of this association, many amulets and religious icons depicting the figure of Christ have been engraved onto bloodstone.

The bloodstone is still considered a healing stone, as it soothes the body, mind, and emotions. It also provides courage, and enables the wearer to face difficult situations in a clear state of mind.

Carnelian

The carnelian is a brownish-red translucent stone that has been used as an amulet since Egyptian times. It was usually carved into the shape of a scarab or a heart. Jewish people engraved seals out of carnelian, and took this stone with them when they left Egypt. In the Arabic tradition, carnelian is used as an amulet to protect the wearer from both the devil and the envious. The prophet Muhammad wore a silver ring set with an engraved carnelian, on the little finger of his right hand.[8] He used it as a seal. Jafar, one of Muhammad's imams (religious leaders), declared that all the desires of people who wore carnelian would be met. During his Egyptian campaign, Napoleon I obtained an octagonal-shaped carnelian seal that was later owned by his nephew Napoleon III. He passed it on to his son, the Prince Imperial, who wore it around his neck. Unfortunately, it disappeared after he was killed by the Zulus in South Africa.

Carnelian is a motivating stone that can help you progress in your life. It helps you maintain total control of your life, and encourages you to achieve more than ever before. It keeps you grounded, and balances your emotions. Because it is so closely connected with the energies of the earth, it is a good stone to use when contacting Uriel.

Moss Agate

The Egyptians were mining agate five and a half thousand years ago, and a large number of beads, rings, and other ornamental objects dating from this time still survive. In his *Natural History,* published in 77 CE, Pliny the Elder claimed that an agate held in the mouth will quench thirst, and that wrestlers who wear agate are invincible.

In the Middle Ages, agate was used as an amulet by business people. This was because it made them eloquent, persuasive, and agreeable to their customers, while at the same time making them closer to God. A sixteenth-century writer called Cardano felt that all forms of agate made their wearers "temperate, continent, and cautious; therefore they are all useful for acquiring riches."[9]

Today, agate is still considered a useful amulet for people in business. It is also used to enhance the connection between the earthly and angelic worlds. Moss agate is particularly useful for contacting Uriel. This is because its gray, brown, and white markings look like moss, providing a double association with the earth element. The earth association also makes the moss agate a good grounding stone, creating a good balance between your intellect and emotions.

Rose Quartz

The delicate pink color of rose quartz may well be responsible for its associations with peace, gentleness, and love. It is a soothing stone that eliminates negative emotional energy. It nurtures its owners by enhancing their self-esteem, and allows them to forgive themselves for any indiscretions they have made in the past.

How to Choose the Right Crystal

You can obtain crystals in many places. If you are adventurous, you may find some good specimens in your explorations. Alternatively, you may be given a suitable stone, or choose one for yourself in a gem store, at a jeweler, or in a new age shop. I find flea markets are often a good source of crystals. Read up on the particular stones that interest you before going on a shopping expedition. You might want to take a book with you, as frequently the staff in lapidary stores are not interested in the spiritual or healing qualities of crystals.

Take your time. Pick up any stones that appeal to you, and see if you experience any sensations while holding them. Give the crystals permission to talk to you, and then listen. You must use your intuition when shopping for crystals. Some stones will seem warm and friendly, while others might appear more distant and cold. Put the stones that respond to you to one side, until you have finished browsing. Then test these stones again, and buy the one that responds best to you.

In practice, I find it hard to do this, and usually end up buying all the stones that I have chosen—or that have chosen me. However, do not buy any stones that you have the slightest doubt about. Frequently, I return from a quest to buy one crystal with a dozen or more, but every now and again I return home with none.

Purification

Once you have your crystal, it needs to be attuned to you and your energies. Although this process is sometimes called "cleansing," it does not mean scrubbing your crystal with soap and water. You can purify your crystal in a number of ways, all of which are effective. You might choose to hold it under cold, running tap water for a minute or two, or perhaps leave it outdoors in the sunlight for a couple hours. Another method is to allow the smoke from incense or burning sage to surround your crystal for a few minutes. However, as this crystal is going to be used to gain a closer connection with Uriel, the best way to purify it is to use the element of earth.

Again, there are a few possibilities. You might choose to bury it in salt overnight. You could also bury it in earth, either outdoors or in a flower pot. Another method is to surround it with other crystals for twenty-four hours.

Once your crystal has been purified, it is almost ready to use. The final stage is to hold it in your hands for at least fifteen minutes. Thirty minutes would be even better. There are two reasons why you should do this. Firstly, it allows the crystal to become thoroughly attuned to you and your energies. Secondly, it gives you some quality time with the crystal. You might choose to meditate during this time, or you may prefer to gently fondle and caress the crystal, and see what messages come to you.

Regardless of how you purify your crystal, you will have to hold it under running water every now and again to remove any dust. After doing this, either dry it with a soft cloth, or let it dry naturally in the sunlight.

How to Dedicate Your Crystal to Uriel

Once your crystal has been purified and is in tune with you, you can dedicate it to Uriel. If the crystal is small enough to hold comfortably, hold it in your hands with the crystal's point upwards. If you are fortunate enough to own a crystal that is too large for this, place it on a table with the point facing upwards, and encircle it with both hands. Naturally, gemstones do not have points in the same way that crystals do. Consequently, it does not matter how you hold them when dedicating them to Uriel.

Sit quietly for a few minutes, and relax yourself as much as possible. If you have worked with your chakras in the past, focus on your crown chakra, and allow it to open. If you have not worked with your chakras before, visualize yourself surrounded by a pure white light. (We will discuss chakras in the next chapter.) You might want to close your eyes to visualize this as clearly as possible. Once you can clearly see or sense the white light, imagine a source of divine energy entering your body through the top of your head and spreading throughout your entire body. Sense it in your fingers and the palms of your hands, and allow this energy to go from you into the crystal, filling it with divine energy.

After you have done this, you need to thank the divine forces for their help and for allowing you to dedicate your crystal for angelic contact. Naturally, it is Uriel in this case, but you can follow the same procedure when dedicating a crystal to any member of the angelic kingdom. You might say:

> *Thank you, God (or Universal Life Force, or whoever else you wish), for filling this crystal with divine energy. I thank you for all your blessings upon me, and request that this crystal be allowed to serve Archangel Uriel. My desire is to be in close contact with Uriel at all times, and I wish this crystal to be so full of his energy that the mere touch of it will put me in immediate contact with him. I hereby dedicate this crystal to the great Archangel Uriel.*

Hold the crystal as high as you can as you say the final sentence. Finally, give thanks one last time to the universal forces, cup the crystal in both hands for a few seconds, and then place it where it will be most useful for you. This is likely to be in a pocket or purse, but you might prefer to place it somewhere where you will see it regularly.

Working with Your Uriel Crystal

The simplest way to work with crystals is to wear or carry one around with you. Ideally, this is a crystal that you have dedicated to Uriel. This enables you to be connected to Uriel's energies all the time. Whenever you feel the need for a close connection with Uriel, all you need do is touch, hold, or caress your Uriel crystal.

Obviously, you should not contact Uriel every five minutes, but you might like to contact him every day to thank him for his help and support. Because he works in a subtle manner, most of the time you will not consciously be aware that he is working on your behalf. It is only when you start noticing that problems that seemed impossible to solve a short while ago have suddenly become minor concerns, that you will realize how much Uriel does for you behind the scenes. Consequently, it is a good habit to thank him on a regular basis.

On the other hand, you should not hesitate to contact him when the need is great or urgent. Carrying a crystal dedicated to Uriel around with you enables you to make instant contact whenever it is necessary.

Working with Crystals

All crystals belong to the earth element, which is Uriel's domain. Consequently, you are making use of his energies whenever you work with crystals. Crystal healers work with many stones. Whether they are aware of it, or not, the stones are all imbued with Uriel's energy. Your connection with Uriel grows whenever you work with crystals or gemstones. Here are some useful ways to work with crystals.

How to Repel Negativity

Some crystals absorb negativity, while others repel it. Tourmaline is a good example of a positive crystal that refuses to accept negativity. It is a wonderful stone to wear, as it also provides feelings of being centered, strong, in control, and relaxed.

Tourmaline comes in a variety of colors, ranging from colorless to black. Blue and red are good choices if you intend to use tourmaline as your Uriel crystal. Dedicate it to Uriel before wearing it.

Once you start wearing tourmaline, you will notice that the anger and negativity of others will cease to have any effect upon you. You will remain calm and relaxed, even if the other person is screaming at you. In fact, the other person will not be able to remain angry for long, as their words will come straight back to them.

Tourmaline also helps eliminate stress and feelings of anxiety. One of my students was plagued by panic attacks until he started wearing tourmaline.

It is interesting to note that Benjamin Franklin was one of a number of people who experimented with the electrical properties of tourmaline. A friend of his in England, Dr. William Haberden, sent him two crystals of tourmaline in June 1759. Benjamin Franklin had one of them "mounted on a pivot on a ring, so that either side could be turned outward at will."[10] In his letter to thank Dr. Haberden for his gift, Franklin mentioned that when he wore the ring, the heat of his finger charged the tourmaline, causing it to attract light bodies. It is not surprising that Benjamin Franklin was intrigued by the properties of tourmaline, as at this time he was involved in important research on the new field of electricity.

Crystal Meditation

It can be highly beneficial to relax and meditate while hold-ing your Uriel crystal. Almost every time I do this, I return from the meditation with new ideas that are relevant to what is going on in my life. This is a good example of Uriel working in mysterious ways, as initially I gave myself credit for the useful ideas. It was only when I realized that these ideas came to me after the meditations were over that I rec-ognized their true source.

I prefer to perform this meditation sitting in a comfort-able chair, as this makes it easier to hold my hands, with the back of my right hand resting on my left palm, and my Uriel crystal resting in my right palm. If you perform the meditation lying down, place the crystal a couple inches above your stomach, cover it with your right hand, and place the left hand on top of it.

Start by closing your eyes and taking several slow, deep breaths. Consciously relax all the muscles in your body, starting at your feet and working your way up to the top of your head.

Once you feel totally relaxed, focus on the crystal you are holding. Become aware of the energy inside it, and wait for a response. You may receive a thought. You might notice a subtle change in the crystal. It may pulse, or seem warmer than it was before. You might feel a sense of overwhelming peace and tranquility. Of course, there will be times when you experience nothing at all. (If you wish, you can use this meditation to contact Uriel. In practice, I prefer to use the other methods that we have already covered.)

Remain in this state for as long as possible. When you notice that your mind is wandering, take a slow, deep breath, count up to five, and open your eyes.

Do not get up immediately. Spend a few minutes thinking about the meditation first. When you feel ready, carry on with your day. For the rest of the day, be alert for good, helpful ideas that suddenly appear in your mind. These are thoughts from Uriel, and you need to think about them carefully and seriously.

Crystal Divination

Uriel has a strong interest in prophecy. If you give readings of any sort, you should ask Uriel for help, as his input will improve your readings immensely. It makes no difference what sorts of readings you give. I have done many different kinds of readings over the years, but have always had a special fondness for crystal readings. It is always pleasant to handle beautiful objects, and the dazzling array of the stones attracts immediate attention. I also enjoy the fact that crystals come from Uriel's element, and feel that he must gain pleasure when people are helped and guided by objects from his realm.

Many years ago, I made a video on crystal divination.[11] This video was aimed at a specific market, and I was unable to include any information about working with angels. However, anyone working with crystals or gemstones for any length of time gradually becomes aware of the angelic influences associated with them, even if they may not realize that it is Uriel's influence that ensures the divinations work.

You will need to collect ninety suitable gemstones. People gasp when I tell them this, but in fact, a collection of gemstones need not cost much more than a good deck of Tarot cards. The stones should all be approximately the same size. Naturally, the size of the stones you buy will depend on how much money you decide to pay. A friend of mine who has written a book on the subject uses stones that are two inches in diameter.[12] Mine are one inch in diameter. The specific stones you choose are not important, but their colors are. You will need ten each of the following colors: red, orange, yellow, green, blue, indigo, violet, rose/pink, and gold. Spend time browsing around lapidary supply stores to find different possibilities. Here are some suggestions:

Red: Garnet, red jasper, ruby, rhodolite, rose quartz

Orange: Carnelian, orange calcite, red aventurine

Yellow: Citrine, yellow beryl, amber, yellow sapphire

Green: Emerald, malachite, jade, green tourmaline

Blue: Lapis lazuli, aquamarine, turquoise, blue sapphire

Indigo: Sodalite, blue tiger-eye

Violet: Amethyst, iolite, sodalite, sugilite

Rose/Pink: Rhodonite, rose quartz, kunzite, pink
tourmaline

Gold: Goldstone, gold tiger-eye, golden beryl

Each of the colors has a specific meaning.

Red

Red is fiery and passionate. It has leadership potential. It is
enthusiastic and energetic. It is often better at starting projects than at finishing them. It is independent, and has
strong needs and desires. In numerology, red relates to the
number one.

Orange

Orange is tactful and diplomatic. It is gentle, intuitive, and
works well with others. It is friendly, cooperative, supportive,
and giving. Orange relates to the number two in numerology.

Yellow

Yellow is joyful, carefree, and fun-loving. It is good at communication and self-expression. It is creative, imaginative,
and positive, and bounces back quickly after setbacks. Yellow relates to the number three in numerology.

Green

Green is capable, practical, conscientious, and hard-working.
It is patient, serious, and rigid in outlook. It has strong likes
and dislikes. Green relates to the number four in numerology.

Blue

Blue is versatile and restless, and enjoys change and variety. It becomes impatient when faced with routine or tedious work. It is enthusiastic and can handle several different tasks at the same time. Blue relates to the number five in numerology.

Indigo

Indigo is responsible, caring, and loving. It is generous, giving, creative, emotional, and appreciative. Indigo loves home and family life. Indigo relates to the number six in numerology.

Violet

Violet is spiritual, studious, and introspective. It works on a different wavelength than the other colors, making it highly original and sometimes unconventional. It needs time on its own to meditate, grow, learn, and understand. Violet relates to the number seven in numerology.

Rose/Pink

Rose/pink is ambitious and a good judge of character. It is reliable, hard-working, practical, and rigid in outlook. It is confident, realistic, and goal-oriented. Rose/pink relates to the number eight in numerology.

Gold

Gold is idealistic, caring, compassionate, and creative. It is sympathetic, tolerant, and giving. It is sensitive and easily hurt. Gold relates to humanitarianism and is always willing to help the underdog.

Now that you know what each gemstone means, you can give yourself a reading. Place all the gemstones in a bag and mix them up. Silently ask Uriel to help you with the divination. When you feel his presence, think of the question you would like to have answered and take out three gemstones, one at a time. Some people like to shake the bag again between each stone. This is a personal preference. Most of the time I don't do this, but occasionally I do. Do what feels right for you at the time. The chances are that you will pick three different colors, but it is possible to pick the same color twice or even all three times.

Let's suppose that you have asked: "Will my marriage improve?" The three gemstones you picked were red, violet, and orange. Using the keywords just given, you see that red is fiery and passionate. As this is the first stone you picked, it is likely to describe the current situation. The next two relate to the future. Violet means that you need time on your own to think about the current situation. Orange is friendly, cooperative, and gets on well with others. This tends to indicate that the marriage will last, and is likely to improve markedly from the current situation.

Here is another example. Let's assume that you asked: "Will I get a pay rise in the next three months?" The gemstones you pick are blue, pink, and green. Blue is restless and wants change and variety. This indicates that you are asking the question because you are feeling unsettled in your work. Pink is hard-working and motivated by goals. It looks as if you'll be working hard in the next few months, and will achieve your goal. Green is patient, practical, and hard-working. It looks as if you will receive your pay rise, but it might take longer than three months to receive it.

The gemstones can help you answer any questions. If it is a simple, relatively straightforward question, one stone might be all that is required. If this does not provide a satisfactory answer, choose another one and see what information it can add to clarify and answer the question.

However, when the question is likely to need more than one stone to answer it, it is better to decide on the number of stones you will use (up to ten), and lay them all out before starting to interpret them.

The stones can also be useful with questions that can be answered with a "yes" or a "no." Shake the stones in the bag, and then put your hand in and grab a handful of stones. Ignore the colors, as it is the number of stones that is important. If you pull out an odd number of stones, the answer is positive. An even number of stones indicates "no."

Reading for Others

You will need Uriel's help when reading for others. Some crystal readers ask him silently, while others like to involve the person for whom they are reading in the process. Do not start the reading until you are sure that he is with you.

Because you have read this far, you know what each stone means. This is why, when you are reading for yourself, you pick the gemstones sight unseen out of a bag. This is not necessary when you are reading for others. Consequently, you might like to make a display of the crystals, and ask the person for whom you are reading to pick up a stone that appeals to them, and to place it on the table to their left. Ask them to choose another stone, which is placed to the right of the first. Ask them to keep on doing this until you have all the stones you feel are necessary to answer the person's question.

Sometimes you will not know what the other person's concerns are. If this is the case, you will have to give them a reading that covers every area of their life. I find that the most practical way of doing this is to use the twelve houses of astrology. Here they are:

- 1st House: Character, personality, and individuality.

- 2nd House: Money and possessions, plus the ability to handle them.

- 3rd House: Brothers and sisters, short trips, communications, and mental aptitudes.

- 4th House: Mother, home, early environment, real estate, and security.

- 5th House: Children, nieces and nephews, pleasure, hobbies, creativity, interests, and love affairs.

- 6th House: Health, work, service to others, food, clothing, and pets.

- 7th House: Partnerships—love, marriage, business, and friendships. Partnerships can also include enemies.

- 8th House: Other people's money—legacies, inheritances, partner's financial affairs, endings, and new beginnings.

- 9th House: Long trips, dreams, visions, intuition, spirituality, intellect, and higher education.

- 10th House: Career, honors, successes, fame, public standing, attainment, and the person's father.

- 11th House: Friends, associations, and hopes, dreams, and wishes for the future.

- 12th House: Secrets, the occult, unforeseen problems.

As you can see, these twelve houses give a comprehensive picture of the person's life and present situation. Have the person for whom you are reading choose twelve stones, one at a time, and place them in a circle. Remember which stone is the first one to be placed down, as that is the one that relates to the first house.

Once all twelve stones have been interpreted, you should ask the person if they would like any further information about any specific area of their life. If they do, ask them to choose three more stones, and interpret them to see what the future indications are.

A friend of mine, who is an extremely gifted crystal reader, uses crystals along with the twelve houses of astrology. However, he uses a completely different method from the one I have just described. He has a large circle, divided into twelve sections, silk-screened onto a table cloth. These represent the twelve houses of astrology. The stones are mixed in a bag, and the person who is to receive the reading places a hand inside the bag, and grabs a handful of stones. The person holds their hand several inches above the center of the circle, and then opens it, allowing the gemstones to drop onto the cloth. The stones that land inside the circle are interpreted according to the houses in which they fall. Any stones that land outside the circle are placed back in the bag, and are not read. My friend invokes Uriel's aid while the stones are being mixed and dropped onto the cloth.

I can understand why he does his readings this way. When an astrology chart is drawn up, the planets are placed in their respective houses. Consequently, there are always houses that contain no planets, while other houses may contain three or four. By dropping the stones onto the circle of houses, the same apparent randomness is created. All the same, I still prefer the first method, as I feel it creates a more complete reading. Experiment with both, and see which method you prefer.

Crystals can be used in many different ways. Experiment, ask Uriel for help, and see what you discover. The combination of crystals and Uriel is a formidable one as far as self-healing and self-knowledge are concerned.

Crystal healers place stones on the chakras to balance them and to facilitate healing. Uriel is the archangel in charge of the solar plexus chakra. We'll learn how to use this knowledge in the next chapter.

Six

———

URIEL AND THE CHAKRAS

CHAKRAS are energy centers inside the aura. The aura is the energy field that surrounds all living things. Chakras are like batteries that help us center and balance our vital energies. They distribute universal, divine energy throughout our bodies. They vitalize and stimulate our physical bodies, and at the same time transmit spiritual energy to help us grow and develop inwardly.

It is important that the chakras are balanced and working correctly. This means that the energy flows easily and smoothly throughout the chakra system. Any blockages or disturbances result in either excessive or deficient energy. These blockages can be caused by emotions such as anger, fear, lust, and jealousy.

There are seven main chakras, aligned along the spinal column, and each is related to one of the endocrine glands. These glands are vital in maintaining energy, stability, and harmony because they provide the necessary hormones to maintain a healthy body.

The word chakra comes from a Sanskrit word that means "wheel" or "disk." Chakras cannot be seen, but they exist in the same way that a thought or emotion does. If a chakra is out of balance for any length of time, a variety of physical effects take place in the physical body.

It is easy to demonstrate this. Have you ever been so full of emotion that your heart felt as if it would burst? That is your heart chakra. Have you ever been so excited that you could not express yourself, and felt that your throat was constricted? That is your throat chakra.

There are seven main chakras. Here they are:

Root Chakra

Location: Base of the spine, coccyx

Element: Earth

Color: Red

Gland: Adrenal

Gemstone: Red coral

Planet: Mars

Archangel: Gabriel

Essential oils: Benzoin, patchouli, vetivert

Functions: Survival, grounding, contact with the earth, physical energy

Sacral Chakra

Location: Four finger-widths below the navel

Element: Water

Color: Orange

Gland: Gonads, prostate

Gemstone: Pearl

Planet: Moon

Archangel: Zadkiel

Essential oils: Dill, geranium, hyssop, jasmine, marjoram, neroli, rose, sandalwood

Functions: Emotions, sexuality

Solar Plexus Chakra

Location: Two finger-widths above the navel

Element: Fire

Color: Yellow

Gland: Pancreas

Gemstone: Ruby

Planet: Sun

Archangel: Uriel

Essential oils: Benzoin, bergamot, chamomile, cypress, dill, elemi, fennel, hyssop, juniper, lemon, marjoram, neroli, sage

Functions: Will, emotional power, intelligence, love, energy, healing, transformation

Heart Chakra

Location: Center of the breastbone

Element: Air

Color: Green

Gland: Thymus

Gemstone: Sapphire

Planet: Venus

Archangel: Chamuel

Essential oils: Benzoin, bergamot, cinnamon, clove, elemi, geranium, immortelle, lavender, lime, mandarin, neroli, palmarose, rose, sandalwood

Functions: Love, family, devotion, balance

Throat Chakra

Location: Throat, at the level of the larynx

Element: Ether

Color: Blue

Gland: Thyroid, parathyroid

Gemstone: Diamond

Planet: Jupiter

Archangel: Michael

Essential oils: Blue chamomile, cajeput, cypress, elemi, eucalyptus, myrrh, palmarose, rosemary, sage, yarrow

Functions: Speaking, communication, creativity, channeling

Third Eye Chakra

Location: Center of forehead, between the eyebrows

Element: Light

Color: Indigo

Gland: Pituitary

Gemstone: Topaz

Planet: Venus

Archangel: Raphael

Essential oils: Basil, carrot seed, clary sage, ginger, Melissa, peppermint, pine, rosemary, rosewood

Functions: Clairvoyance, imagination

Crown Chakra

Location: Top of the head

Element: Thought

Color: Violet

Gland: Pineal

Gemstone: Emerald

Planet: Saturn

Archangel: Jophiel

Essential oils: Cedarwood, elemi, frankincense, jasmine, neroli, rose, rosewood

Functions: Spirituality, intuition, illumination, understanding, inner knowledge

The Solar Plexus Chakra

As you can see, Uriel has an interest in the solar plexus chakra. This chakra is the center of a person's personal power. When the person feels happy and fulfilled, his ego and self-esteem will be nourished and used in a positive manner. It is the chakra of self-acceptance and intelligence. When this is channeled, the conscious and unconscious minds are harmonized, endowing the person with creativity and unique insights.

Fear is the main enemy of this chakra. When the person feels fearful, he is denying his own personal power. He will try to please others, at considerable personal cost, and is likely to experience digestive problems. Frequently, fear can be felt in the area of the solar plexus chakra. The quickest remedy for this is to take several deep breaths, as our breathing tends to become shallow and rapid when we are afraid. Deep breaths also help eliminate butterflies in the stomach.

This chakra is also involved with metabolism, the process that transforms food into energy. Digestive, stomach, and weight problems all indicate that this chakra is not balanced and working the way it should.

How we feel about ourselves is indicated by this chakra. Consequently, it has a huge effect on every aspect of our lives, from choosing a career to sustaining a relationship. Obviously, if we feel good about ourselves, we can achieve much more than when we don't.

Fear closes down the solar plexus chakra. This makes the person timid, withdrawn, and lacking in energy. This person will avoid confrontation, and will have a fear of taking risks. Life will be a grim and serious business.

Of course, the opposite scenario applies if this chakra is too open. In this case, the person will want to control every situation, and will be aggressive, domineering, self-centered, and concerned only with her own gratification.

Ideally, the solar plexus chakra should be healthy and balanced. This produces someone who is aware of her own power, but uses it appropriately. This person has good self-esteem, and will stand up for herself, will act when necessary, will finish tasks, and will be fair and considerate to others.

The best way to energize your solar plexus chakra is to do something physical. A brisk walk or jog stimulates this chakra, and helps all the other chakras, too. Laughing and having a good time is another effective method of strengthening and energizing this chakra.

Gemstones can be used to strengthen this chakra, too. Crystal healers place stones over the chakras when working on their clients. The stones that relate to the solar plexus chakra are amber, citrine, golden topaz, green and yellow tourmaline, heliodore, picture jasper, and tiger-eye.

Solar Plexus Chakra Energizer

As your solar plexus chakra is the seat of your vitality and energy, you should ensure that it is kept fully charged and vibrant. Here is a simple exercise that enables you to do this. This exercise also expands your aura.

1. Sit down comfortably, close your eyes, and take several deep breaths. Visualize yourself surrounded by a pure, clear light, and breathe this energy in

each time you inhale. Gradually allow every muscle in your body to relax.

2. When you feel fully relaxed, visualize yourself standing in front of a large mirror. As you look at yourself in the mirror, allow the years to fall away until you see yourself as you were when you were twenty years old. You are naked, and can see how fit and vital you were then. You also notice the pure white light that completely surrounds your reflection.

3. Look at your solar plexus in the mirror, and take a slow, deep breath. Feel it being absorbed into your solar plexus chakra, and sense a wave of vibrant energy coursing through your entire body. Repeat this several times, until you feel yourself full of revitalizing energy and power.

4. Invite Uriel to join you. It is possible that you will see him in the mirror, but it is more likely that you will become aware of his presence. Ask him to check your solar plexus chakra to ensure that it is energized and in balance. Thank him if he tells you that the chakra is working properly. However, if he tells you that it is not yet properly balanced, repeat step 3, and then ask him again. Continue doing this until Uriel gives you a positive response.

5. Allow yourself to slowly return to your present age, and notice how much better you look now than

you did when you started the exercise. You look and feel vibrant and full of life. You have restored your energy levels, and are ready for anything.

6. Allow the image of the mirror to fade, and become aware of where you are. Take a moment to thank the universal forces for enabling you to have all the energy you need, and when you feel ready, open your eyes.

The Root Chakra

You may have noticed that although the Archangel Uriel is associated with the solar plexus chakra, this chakra has fire as its element. The root chakra has earth as its element. Consequently, many people relate Uriel to the root chakra rather than the solar plexus chakra.

I have had many discussions with people about this, and feel that although it may seem confusing, Uriel's relationship with two chakras is highly beneficial. It means that you can ask him for help in any matters relating to either of them.

The root chakra, situated at the base of the spine, is concerned with survival, and anything relating to that. It is only once our survival needs have been met that we can start focusing on anything else. Recently, I read an article about an art gallery that had opened in Kabul, Afghanistan. The owners were finding it extremely difficult to attract customers, as almost everyone in Kabul is concerned solely with survival. Once those needs are taken care of, they will be able to spend time on other aspects of life, including culture.

Even in the superficially prosperous and stable Western world, we can still experience threats to our survival. If you suddenly lose your job or have to move to another apartment, for instance, you could easily upset the balance of your root chakra. Interestingly enough, eating disorders are often a root chakra concern. We need to eat to survive, of course, but when people eat either too much or too little, they are experiencing an imbalance in the root chakra. Many people feel uncomfortable, insecure, unaccepted, or paranoid. These are all indications that the root chakra is not in balance.

The root chakra plays a vital role in the will to live. If you have ever experienced the "fight or flight" response, which comes from the adrenal glands, then you know how essential the root chakra is to life.

If you ever feel insecure, or are constantly coping with threats to your way of life, ask Uriel for help.

Root Chakra Energizer

All of the chakras need to be looked after. Arguably, the root chakra is the most important as it is concerned with life itself. Fortunately, it is an easy manner to energize it.

1. Sit down in a straight-backed chair, with both feet flat on the floor. The angle at your knees should be

approximately ninety degrees, and your back should be resting comfortably against the back of the chair. Push your feet downwards into the floor, and you will feel your buttocks and thighs move. This stimulates the root chakra. Do this three or four times, holding the push downwards for a few seconds each time.

2. Close your eyes, and push downwards one last time. Relax and focus on your root chakra. You will feel or sense a response. It is likely to be a tingling feeling at the base of your spine. However, people experience things in different ways, and your response might not be the same as mine. People I have spoken to have experienced such varied sensations as warmth, cold, vibration, and even the sense that something heavy is sitting in that position.

3. Call on Uriel and ask him to energize your root chakra. Once he starts doing this, the sensation will be stronger than before. Instead of a delicate tingle, the response is more likely to be a pulsation. When he stops, you will feel a sense of grounding and solidity, and will feel in control of your life again.

4. Visualize a clear white light descending and enveloping you in its glow. You may feel it enter your body at the top of your head and travel down through each chakra until it reaches your root chakra.

5. When you feel ready to carry on with your day, thank Uriel for his assistance. Take three slow, deep breaths, and open your eyes. Your root chakra is now energized, and you should feel ready for anything.

Chakra Massage

This exercise enables you to energize each of the chakras. It is a restful, restorative exercise that will improve every area of your life. I frequently give myself a chakra massage while lying in bed at night, but it can be done at any time. You will find it so beneficial that you will probably want to do it every day.

1. Sit or lie down comfortably. Take a few deep breaths and relax yourself as much as possible.

2. When you feel ready, visualize yourself standing on the stage of a large theatre. The theatre is full of people, and you are happy they are there, as they have come to support you. You feel perfectly comfortable and at ease on the stage. The stage is unlit, except for a single spotlight that slowly moves around and highlights different parts of the stage. After a minute or two, it finds you. It stops moving, and you stand in the middle of the circle of light.

3. You gaze up at the light, and realize that Uriel is operating the light. As you think about this, you

become aware that the light is not simply high-lighting you on the stage. It is also surrounding you with a clear, healing glow. You also notice that while the light from the spotlight comes from above you, there is also an equivalent light shining upwards from beneath you.

4. You feel your body absorbing the energy from the two light sources, and you hear Uriel telling you to become aware of your root chakra. You focus on the base of your spine, and sense a ball of pure red energy expanding and contracting as it gives your root chakra a massage.

5. After a minute, this red ball of energy disappears, and you notice that it has been replaced by a ball of orange energy that massages your sacral chakra.

6. This is replaced in turn by balls of yellow, green, blue, indigo, and violet energy that massage each of the chakras in turn.

7. After the final ball of energy disappears, you feel the light from each source strengthen momentar-ily as they both change from a clear light to white. You realize that this is the final stage of the mas-sage, and that the white light is balancing and har-monizing all of your chakras. You stretch luxuri-ously, and smile at the people in the audience. They applaud and cheer as they gaze at the com-pletely restored and revitalized you.

8. You look up and thank Uriel for the massage, and for his love and dedication. Both light sources flicker slightly, as if acknowledging your thanks. Then Uriel turns them off, and you find yourself back in your everyday world.

9. If you are doing this exercise in bed at night, roll over and enjoy a good night's sleep. You will find the chakra massage extremely restful. If you are doing this massage at any other time, stretch, and open your eyes when you feel ready. Nothing will bother or disturb you for the rest of the day. Any stress or tension will simply fall away, having no effect upon you. Many of my students have commented that this exercise also helps bolster their self-esteem.

Chakra Balancing

Your chakras should be in balance and working efficiently all the time. Of course, in practice, this is not always possible. Something as simple as a car cutting you off in traffic might be enough to upset the balance of your chakras. The chakra massage exercise balances your chakras. Another way of doing this is to imagine yourself walking through a rainbow, becoming totally surrounded and engulfed by each color in turn.

There will be times, though, when you are aware that your chakra system is not working as efficiently as it should be, and you will want to know which chakra (or chakras) is out of balance. The easiest way to do this is to use a pendulum.

A pendulum is a small weight attached to a thread or chain. You can buy dowsing pendulums at new age stores, but almost anything will do. I have used a paperclip attached to a piece of thread, when nothing else was available. At one time I used to carry a pendulum with me everywhere I went. However, as my favorite pendulum was made of an alloy of different metals, since 9/11 I have had problems with it at airline metal detectors, and no longer carry it.

Pendulums are easy to use. Hold the thread between the thumb and first finger of your dominant hand, and allow the weight to hang freely. You might like to rest your elbow on a table, and have the weight hanging about an inch above the table's surface.

Stop the movements of the pendulum with your free hand, and then ask your pendulum to move in a direction that indicates "yes." There are four possibilities: it will move from side to side, towards and away from you, or in a circular motion, either clockwise or counterclockwise.

If you have not used a pendulum before, it might take a few minutes before it moves for the first time. However, you will quickly find that with just a little practice, the pendulum will start moving as soon as you ask a question.

Once you have determined which movement indicates "yes," ask it for the movements that indicate "no," "I don't know," and "I don't want to answer." Now you can ask it questions about each chakra.

Start by asking if your chakras are balanced. If the answer is yes, you can put the pendulum away and carry on with your day. However, it is more likely to indicate that one or more of your chakras are out of balance.

There are many ways to rebalance the chakras that are out of balance. One method involves the pendulum. Focus on the chakra that is out of balance. If possible, actually feel the chakra in your mind. While doing this, make the pendulum swing vigorously in a clockwise direction. This is called "winding." After sixty seconds, stop, and test the result with your pendulum. Continue doing this until the pendulum gives a positive response.

Another method is to focus on each chakra in turn. You will experience a slight tingling feeling with each chakra as you do this. Focus on your root chakra, and breathe in deeply. Visualize this breath going directly to your root chakra, filling it with energy. Exhale slowly, turning the exhalation into a long, deep sigh. Use your pendulum to see if this chakra is now balanced. Repeat, if necessary, until you receive a positive response. Repeat with each of the chakras in turn.

Chakra Balancing with Uriel

Earlier on, I mentioned that you should not bother Uriel with matters that you can resolve on your own. Most of the time, you will be able to balance your chakras without Uriel's help.

However, you can call on him for help, if you do ever experience problems.

Stand, with your feet slightly apart and your arms by your sides. Close your eyes, take a few deep breaths, and then ask Uriel to join you. When you sense his presence, tell him your chakras are out of balance and need to be attended to.

Visualize yourself standing in the center of a circle of pure white light that provides you with energy and protection while Uriel balances your chakras. You may, or may not, experience sensations in the areas of your chakras as he works, but you will sense a feeling of strength and confidence as soon as he has finished. Thank him for his help, take three more deep breaths, and then open your eyes.

Opening and Closing Your Chakras

There will be times when you want your chakras to be open and receptive. If you want to become more aware or intuitive, for instance, your chakras must be open to allow impressions to come in. Likewise, your chakras should be open when you are receiving a spiritual or psychic healing. However, if you find yourself in a difficult or negative environment, you may want to temporarily close your chakras down to prevent the negativity from entering your system.

Ideally, your chakras should be in a state of balance. It is not a good idea to keep them completely open or closed for any length of time. This can affect your health, as the chakras balance and harmonize your emotional and psychic energy.

You can open and close your chakras quickly. To open your chakras, visualize a wave of pure energy coming up from the ground and working its way through your body, gently stimulating and opening each chakra as it goes.

To close down your chakras, do the same thing in reverse. Visualize the wave of energy starting at your crown chakra and working its way down your spine and finally down to the ground where the energy is absorbed.

If you have established instant communication with Uriel, you might prefer to ask him to open or close your chakras.

You may want to close down just one or two chakras. You can do this by visualizing your body, with the chakras in position, all glowing with their respective colors. Mentally, turn off, or dim, the light in the chakra you wish to close. Once the situation you are in is over, you can turn the light back on again.

Obviously, it is important to rebalance your chakras again after opening or closing them. Although you can do this in a matter of seconds, it is a good idea to nurture yourself by taking as much time as you wish to restore your chakra system to balance.

Essential Oils and the Chakras

Angels enjoy pleasant fragrances. Consequently, they are frequently used to attract angelic forces. They also heighten our consciousness and awareness, making us more receptive and open to angelic communication.

Many people have noticed that they become aware of an unbelievably beautiful scent shortly before an angelic appearance. This otherworldly scent often lingers for thirty or forty minutes after the angel has gone.

Essential oils are healing and restorative. At the same time, they allow spiritual growth to occur. This is why they are so useful in angelic communication. Essential oils are more popular today than ever before because they are used in the important area of holistic medicine known as aromatherapy.

Essential oils can be obtained from a variety of places, including herb stores, new age stores, gift shops, and some pharmacies. There are specific oils that relate strongly to different chakras, and these are listed in the keywords for each chakra, at the start of this chapter. You will find it helpful to use these when working on a specific chakra, or if you are contacting the archangel who relates to a specific chakra. However, you should also experiment with the different oils, as it is important that you like the scents you use. Consequently, I have listed several essential oils for each chakra.

Here are some of the best-known essential oils that can be used for angelic contact:

Angelica Seed

Angelica seed probably got its name because of its strong association with the angelic realms. It helps you open up your intuition, and has been known to help people who have lost their faith.

Benzoin

Benzoin is a protective oil that relates particularly well to Archangel Michael. It helps you open up the heart chakra.

Bergamot

Bergamot is closely connected with Archangel Jophiel. It is used to gain a closer connection with the spiritual realms. It provides a sense of joy, light, and confidence.

Chamomile

Chamomile is a good oil to use with Archangel Uriel, as it brings comfort, healing, and peace to those who need it. It allows you to let go of anger and resentment, and remain calm and relaxed at all times. It also allows you to forgive others more easily.

Cypress

Cypress relates well to Uriel, and should be used whenever you are going through a transition period in your life. It gives strength, peace of mind, and acceptance.

Elemi

Elemi opens up channels to the divine. It provides comfort, protection, love, and contentment. It should be used whenever you feel the need for peace.

Fennel

Fennel provides strength of character, and the ability to stand up for oneself in difficult situations. It provides energy and courage.

Hyssop

Hyssop should be used by anyone who requires purification of body, mind, and/or spirit. It eliminates feelings of negativity, guilt, and fear. It is especially useful for victims of any form of abuse.

Juniper

Juniper cleanses and purifies the body, mind, and spirit, and allows forgiveness to take place. It helps people work through past traumas and start again, with a positive outlook and good self-esteem. It also provides protection when necessary.

Lemon

Lemon is a cleansing oil that relates well to Archangel Michael. It allows the person to look at life with new eyes, and provides confidence, vitality, and a revitalized faith.

Marjoram

Marjoram relates to Archangel Raphael, and is especially useful for people who cannot find peace of mind. It calms restless people, and allows them to find peace, quiet, and contentment.

Neroli

People who find it hard to learn from their mistakes should use neroli. It provides joy, stimulation, and a greater sense of what life is about. It is highly attractive to all the angelic realms.

Palmarosa

Palmarosa should be used by anyone who has suffered a knock to their self-esteem or confidence. It helps provide feelings of self-worth, and a desire to make progress in the future.

Patchouli

Patchouli provides emotional peace, and eases difficult, stressful situations. It provides energy, and a sense that you can handle anything that life hands you. Stress often has an adverse effect on the libido, and patchouli helps reverse this.

Sage

Sage opens up the aura, allowing spiritual progress to occur. It helps balance the physical and emotional bodies. It is useful if you are searching for a new direction in life.

Vetiver

Vetiver allows you to renew yourself mentally and emotionally. It grounds you, allowing you to regain your connection with the earth, and let go of everyone else's problems.

Wisteria

Wisteria is sometimes known as "poet's ecstasy," as it stimulates creativity. It is also useful for inspirational and spiritual growth. It helps provide insights into areas that may have been bothering or concerning you for some time.

How to Use the Essential Oils

By far the easiest, and safest, method of using essential oils is to use an electric oil burner that can be obtained anyplace where aromatherapy supplies are sold. These burners create just the right amount of heat to allow the essential oil to release its scent. All you need do is add eight to ten drops of the oil to the burner before turning it on.

Alternatively, you might choose to use a more traditional oil burner that is heated by a candle. Naturally, this should never be left unsupervised.

If you feel the need for a rapid dose of the scent, add up to ten drops of oil to a bowl of steaming water. Place a towel over your head and the bowl, and inhale the scent in the vapor for a few minutes.

You can also add a drop or two of an essential oil to a handkerchief, pillow, or shirt collar. Most essential oils will not cause a stain, although you should be careful with the darker-colored ones, such as vetiver or patchouli.

The next chapter continues our research into the Archangel of the Earth, as we start using crystals in a different way. Dr. John Dee and Edward Kelley communicated with Uriel, and many other angels, with a crystal ball. Scrying, as this method of divination is known, is the subject of the next chapter.

Seven

SCRYING FOR URIEL

DURING the eighteenth and nineteenth centuries, a large number of grimoires and other magic books appeared. Often the authors claimed that the works had been published hundreds of years earlier. One example of this is the *Grimorium Verum*. The title page reads:

> Grimorium Verum, or the Most Approved Keys of Solomon the Hebrew Rabbin, wherein the Most Hidden Secrets, both Natural and Supernatural, are immediately exhibited; but it is necessary that the Demons should be contented on their part. Translated from the Hebrew by Plaingière, a Dominican Jesuit, with a Collection of Curious Secrets. Published by Alibeck the Egyptian. 1517.

However, despite the year, the *Grimorium Verum* dates back only to the middle of the eighteenth century. The page after the title page also states that the publisher was based in Memphis. In fact, he was in Rome.[1]

Further difficulties can also be found on the title page. A "Dominican Jesuit" does not exist, as the Order of Saint Dominic and the Society of Jesus are completely different organizations, even though they are both part of the Roman Catholic Church.

Also, the translation of the wording on the title page is partly conjecture, as some of the Latin makes no sense at all. This is also true of parts of the text.

The *Grimorium Verum,* like many other grimoires of the period, is based partly on the better-known *Key of Solomon,* which is a strange mixture of both black and white magic. The first part of the *Grimorium Verum* concerns conjuring up demons, but the second part contains "Rare and Astounding Magical Secrets," which include a detailed description on how to induce clairvoyance. It also includes a ritual called the Word or Speech of Uriel. In this ritual, Uriel is ceremonially invoked, and then proceeds to answer questions. The version outlined in the *Grimorium Verum* requires two people, but this is not essential. You can perform this ritual on your own.

The *Grimorium Verum* states that for the ritual to work, it should be held in a small room that has not been occupied by "impure women" for at least nine days. The room needs to be thoroughly cleansed and consecrated. A table, covered with a clean white cloth, is placed in the center of the room. On this are placed a glass full of spring water, three small candles of virgin wax, which have been mixed with human fat, a six-inch-square sheet of parchment paper, a china inkwell that has been filled with fresh ink, a pen, and a pan containing materials for a small fire. Also required is a nine- or ten-year-old boy, who needs to be well behaved and modestly dressed.

The candles are attached to needles, six inches behind, and on both sides of the glass of water. While putting these in position, the magician must recite the following words: "Gabamiah, Adonay, Agla, O Lord God of Powers, do Thou assist us!"

The parchment is placed on the right side of the glass of water, and the pen and ink are placed to the left. The doors and windows of the room are then closed, and the candles and fire lit. The ritual can now begin.

The boy joins his hands together, kneels in front of the glass of water, and gazes into it. The magician moves to the boy's right-hand side and says the following conjuration:

"Uriel, Seraph, Josata, Ablati, Agla, Caila, I pray and conjure thee by the Four Words which God uttered with His mouth unto His servant Moses, Josata, Ablati, Agla, Caila, and by the Nine Heavens wherein thou dwellest, as also by the virginity of this child who is before thee, that thou appearest, and without any delay, visibly in this phial (glass), to discover, without disguising, the truth which I desire to know; which done, I will discharge thee in peace and goodwill, in the Name of the Most Holy Adonay."

The boy is then asked if he sees anything in the glass. If he sees an angel, or any other apparition, in the water, the magician welcomes it, and then asks the vision to answer questions relating to the purpose of the ritual. The angel can respond in three ways. He can communicate with the boy clairvoyantly, speak to the magician in his dreams, or write down the answers on the sheet of parchment. After the ritual is finished, the room is sealed until the following morning, which gives the angel sufficient time to write a message on the parchment.

Naturally, the angel is listened to, if he chooses to communicate through the boy. If the angel fails to do this, the magician repeats his request twice more, and then puts out the candles and leaves the room, confident that he will have the answers to his questions the following morning.

The method of scrying outlined here is similar to the methods used by Dr. John Dee and Edward Kelley. Kelley would gaze into a cauldron of water, or a shew-stone, while John Dee wrote down the visions that Kelley saw. John Dee's shew-stone is a quartz crystal ball, and it can be seen in the Gallery of Enlightenment at the British Museum in London.

Archangel Uriel was probably chosen for this particular ritual, as he is the archangel responsible for prophecy. However, you can use this ritual to contact any of the archangels, if you wish.

Scrying is an ancient method of divination. Crystal ball gazing is a good example. However, a glass of water works just as well. All you need do is gaze deeply into the glass of water and see what images come into your mind. It is not usual for the images to appear inside the glass or crystal ball, although this can occur. Most of the time, vivid impressions will come into your mind.

If you would like to communicate with Uriel in this way, use a clean glass tumbler that is free of patterns or other markings. Fill it almost to the top with fresh drinking water, and place it on a table covered with a white cloth. The cloth needs to be white, as any patterns or colors in the cloth could have an adverse effect on the scrying. Use three candles, if you wish. There is no need to prepare candles out of virgin wax and human fat. All you need are three good-quality candles.

Obviously, you must have a reason for contacting Uriel. Have your goal clearly in mind before you start. The room also needs to be clean and freshly aired.

Do something to separate yourself from your normal everyday life. If you intend to scry in the evening, eat lightly and avoid alcohol and other stimulants beforehand. Go for a walk, listen to a favorite piece of music, or do something else that you find enjoyable for an hour or so before starting the ritual. Follow this with a shower or bath, and change into clean clothes. I like to brush my teeth, as well. Once you have done this, you are ready to begin.

Sit down comfortably in front of the glass of water, so that your eyes are about eighteen inches away from the glass. Some authorities claim that the best results come when you face east. However, as you are contacting Uriel, you might prefer to face north. Experiment, and see which direction produces better results for you.

Gaze into the glass, and say a prayer to Uriel, asking him to come to your aid. You might say: "Uriel, Light of God, please help me. I am having difficulties with [state the problem as clearly as possible]. I need your peace and understanding. Fill me with your tranquility, knowledge, and love. Please come to me, Uriel."

Edward Kelley sometimes felt a physical touch on his head or shoulder at this stage in the ritual, which was the angels alerting him to their presence.[2]

Wait for between thirty and sixty seconds to see if you receive any response. You may feel a gentle touch, or sense Uriel's presence. You may see him in the water of the glass. You may hear from him clairaudiently. Once you receive a response, no matter what it is, you can start talking to him, either in your mind or out loud.

Even if the initial contact did not come through the glass of water, keep gazing into it, as visions may well appear in your mind. Keep communicating for as long as necessary. There is no need to draw out the procedure.

Naturally, you must finish by thanking Uriel for coming to your aid. You might say something along these lines: "Uriel, Light of God, thank you for releasing me from my fears. Thank you for filling me with your peace and love. Thank you for your kindness, loyalty, and willingness to help. I appreciate everything you do for me. Thank you, Archangel Uriel, thank you."

Stay seated for a minute or two, thinking about what has occurred. You may want to make some notes about the experience. When you feel ready to continue with your day, take a slow, deep breath and exhale slowly. Put out the candles, if you used them, and pour out the water from the glass, thanking it for helping you in the ritual as you do so.

Of course, there will be occasions when Uriel does not appear to respond to your call. If this happens, repeat your call twice more, and then give up for the day. Most of the time, when this happens, the answer you seek will come to you in your sleep, and you will not need to repeat the ritual on the following day. Repeat the ritual, if necessary, until you make contact.

Like everything else, your skills at scrying will develop with practice. Be patient if you fail to make contact the first time, or even the first dozen times, you perform this ritual. Scrying is a particularly useful talent to develop. Some people are successful on their first attempt at scrying, but most people have to develop the skill through regular practice. This skill is so useful that any amount of time spent practicing it will prove well worthwhile.

You may choose to continue scrying with a glass of water. However, if you particularly enjoy scrying, you should also experiment with a crystal ball and a crystal mirror. Both of these should be available at new age stores. Crystal balls come in a variety of sizes. Obviously, the larger ones are more expensive. If the store has several to choose from, take your time and test each ball before deciding on the one to buy.

Many scryers prefer to use a mirror, in preference to a crystal ball. You can scry with any mirror. However, most mirror scryers use a special black mirror that is manufactured for the purpose. These were originally made from obsidian, but any reasonably shiny black surface will do. They were popular in Victorian times, but then almost disappeared from view. Fortunately, a number of people have started making them again. Consequently, if you have a large store near you, you will be able to test a number of mirrors before deciding on the one that appeals most to you.

Eight

HOW TO INTRODUCE
URIEL TO OTHERS

YOU will find that your regular communications with Uriel play an increasingly important role in your life. The quality of your life will steadily improve once you develop a relationship with him. As a result of this, your friends and acquaintances are likely to start asking questions about the changes they see in you. Consequently, you will probably want to tell others about Uriel. It is a wonderful thing to help other people improve their lives, but you should exercise caution.

Not everyone will approve of your interest in the angelic kingdom, and you might be accused of all sorts of bizarre behavior. I have relatives who do not like the subject matter of my books. As I have to spend time with them at family occasions, I find it better not to discuss any projects I happen to be working on. If they were to express interest, I would be delighted to talk about them. However, for the sake of family harmony, I find it better not to broach the subject.

Other people will have fears about dabbling into something that they consider occult. Despite the fact that you are communicating with angels, some people will still consider what you are doing to be satanic. Some will have had unpleasant experiences in the past and be wary about exploring anything new.

One woman I know keeps well away from any psychic or spiritual groups because of an experience she had many years ago. She belonged to a group that was concerned about the future of the earth, and performed numerous rituals outdoors. One of the other members of the group continually suggested that they perform the rituals naked. She felt uneasy about this, and left the group because she doubted his motives. Her feelings turned out to be correct, and the group split into a number of factions, and ultimately disbanded.

The people you meet regularly will notice changes in you once you start working with angels. If they ask questions about this, you should explain that you are working with Uriel, and briefly tell them what you are doing. Their response to this will tell you whether or not to pursue the subject.

I find it helpful to mention Uriel to people who are dealing with problems that fall into Uriel's areas of interest. I would, for instance, be likely to tell someone who was forever giving, but receiving little or no gratitude in return, about Uriel. I would tell her anything she wanted to know, but it would then be up to that person to contact Uriel, if she wished. I would do the same for someone who was attempting to find inner peace.

If someone was tackling a creative project, or was trying to master a particular divination technique, I would talk to them about Uriel, as that would enable them to progress much more quickly.

It would be harder to do this with people who were full of anger, or who do things only for personal gain. In a situation like this, it would probably be better to talk about angels in general, and see what response you receive, before starting to talk about Uriel.

In practice, I never force my beliefs onto other people. I am happy to talk about my views and beliefs with others at any time, and am equally as happy to listen to what they have to say. Unfortunately, there are many people who want to push their views down my throat, but have no interest in my perspective on the subject. In situations like this, nothing is gained by arguing about the matter, and it is better to walk away.

Fortunately, you will meet many people who are interested in the angelic kingdom, and you will receive enormous pleasure from helping them. Some of these people may want to take their interest further, and you will have the opportunity to form a group of like-minded people. You will then have to decide whether to include them in your rituals.

Forming a Ritual Group

All you need is one other person to form a ritual group. Be alert for other people who might be interested, but do not accept anyone without determining their level of interest beforehand.

Decide on how regularly you will meet. You might decide to have a study session one evening a week. You might decide to meet at each full moon, or at the eight sabbats. I find it best to ask each member to commit to a certain number of meetings, such as an eight-week study course, and then ask them if they want to continue for a further eight weeks. Someone needs to be appointed to the task of reminding everyone a day or two ahead of the upcoming meeting, so that people do not accidentally miss any. One group I was involved with at one time sent formal invitations to each member, inviting them to attend. They felt that specially prepared invitations were necessary to stress the importance of their meetings.

Someone should be appointed leader of the group for a while, but you are likely to have better results if you share the leadership, with each person having responsibility for certain tasks. If you are performing rituals on the sabbats, for instance, you might have one person arranging and organizing the first one, while another person does the second, and so on. This keeps everyone involved and interested, and allows them to use their own flair and creativity. Obviously, mistakes will be made, but this does not matter as long as lessons are learned from them.

You might have a meeting to discuss a name for your group. You should also have meetings to discuss the formats of the different rituals you intend to perform. You will also need to discuss the theme of the ritual, and prepare for it accordingly.

Membership also needs consideration. You will need meetings to discuss the merits of prospective members. Some groups consist of a single sex, while others accept men and women. I prefer mixed groups, but can understand why some people prefer to belong to a group that consists of just one sex.

Different matters, such as choice of venue, clothing, and items that will be needed for the ritual, all need to be discussed. These should all be determined ahead of time to avoid frustrations, mistakes, and delays on the night. Someone should be appointed record-keeper, to keep detailed notes of each ritual.

One group I belonged to had an official photographer. I wasn't happy with this, as I thought it would prove disruptive. However, he took no photographs during the rituals. Instead, he took plenty of photographs before and after, and also photographed reenactments of different parts of the rituals. His photographs built up a valuable record of the group.

This particular group had thirty members, and everyone had specific responsibilities. One knowledgeable person fulfilled the role of Educator, and gave talks and workshops a day or two ahead of each ritual, to make sure that every participant knew the relevance and history of the particular ritual. If the ritual was to commemorate Halloween, for instance, he would research it in depth and tell the group about his findings. He would also tell the members what the group had done on previous Halloweens and ask for suggestions for the ritual this year.

Someone else was the Wardrobe Mistress. Despite the old-fashioned, sexist title, the man who fulfilled this role enjoyed storing and looking after the different-colored robes that this group used. The Historian recorded every meeting, filling up several books with valuable information. Another person was responsible for procuring and looking after the candles. Someone else looked after the crystals, and her husband had the unenviable task of looking after and transporting the twelve rocks that were used to create the circle within which the group worked.

Someone else searched the countryside for suitable places to perform the rituals. On one memorable occasion, we performed a ritual inside the crater of an extinct volcano at daybreak. Much to our surprise, another group had chosen the same venue, and we worked together to create a large celebration to welcome in the new season.

This group also did something that I have seldom seen elsewhere. When a new member came to be initiated into the group, the person was welcomed at a special ritual, which was held separately from any other ritual. Everyone wore white robes, to symbolize the new beginning. The initiate sat in the middle of the circle, surrounded by the existing members. He was welcomed into the group by each member individually, who went up to the initiate, kissed him, whispered something in his ear, and gave him a small gift, such as an orange or a gemstone. The person who had introduced the initiate then stood up and gave his or her reasons for inviting the person to join, and then the leader for the night formally welcomed the initiate into the group.

Although this group is larger than most, everyone has a vital role to play. Everyone also has a turn at leading the group. I think the combination of individual responsibilities, combined with a leadership role every now and again, plays a major part in the survival of this group, which has now been operating for more than twenty years. This group is a pagan one, and has nothing to do with archangels. I have used it as an example here, as it shows how a small group can grow in both number and maturity as time goes on.

You may have no interest in setting up a group of this sort at present. However, you never know when you might chance across some like-minded people, and start meeting informally. Keep it casual and lighthearted at first, but as you gain new members, you will need to establish some sort of structure if you want the group to survive.

Nine

THE OTHER
ARCHANGELS

MICHAEL, Gabriel, Raphael, and Uriel are the best-known archangels in the Christian tradition. April 20th is the Feast of the Seven Angels, indicating the long-standing belief that there are seven archangels. Seven angels are mentioned in both the book of Revelation (8:2) and the book of Tobit (12:15), but neither source lists their names. Over the last two thousand years, many people have come up with suggestions.

In the first book of Enoch, Enoch named them as Uriel, Raguel, Michael, Saraqâêl, Gabriel, Remiel, and Raphael. In the third book of Enoch, he changed the list to read: Michael, Gabriel, Satqiel, Sahaqiel, Baradiel, Barqiel, and Sidriel. Other lists can be found in the *Apocrypha* and a variety of the books in the *Pseudopigrapha*. In these, the following archangels are mentioned: Anael, Barachiel, Jehudiel, Sealtiel, Oriphiel, and Zadkiel.

In Islam, four archangels are recognized, but only two are mentioned by name in the Koran. They are Gabriel (Jibril) and Michael. The unnamed archangels are Azrael, the angel of death, and Israfil, the angel of music. Israfil is the angel who, in the Islamic tradition, will sound the trumpet on Judgment Day.

Although there are only the four archangels in Muslim lore, most sources list seven.[1] This is partly because seven has always been considered a mystical number, but also because in the Bible we read: ". . . the seven princes of Persia and Media, which saw the king's face, and which sat the first in the kingdom." (Esther 1:14) Another possibility is that the ancient Babylonians regarded the seven planets as deities, and consequently assumed that there would also be seven archangels.

Not surprisingly, each day of the week is represented by an archangel. In *The Magus,* Francis Barrett offered this listing:[2]

Sunday: Michael

Monday: Gabriel

Tuesday: Camael (Chamuel)

Wednesday: Raphael

Thursday: Sachiel (Zadkiel)

Friday: Anael

Saturday: Cassiel

There are also archangels who look after each sign of the zodiac, listed here:

Aries: Saraquael

Taurus: Ashmodiel

Gemini: Ambriel

Cancer: Cael

Leo: Zerachiel

Virgo: Vael

Libra: Zuriel

Scorpio: Baruel

Sagittarius: Adnachiel

Capricorn: Orphiel

Aquarius: Cambiel

Pisces: Barakiel

Naturally, there are also angels for each of the planets. In the Kabbalistic and medieval magic traditions, the seven traditional planets were assigned angels, and new angels were added to the list as other planets were discovered:

Sun: Michael

Moon: Gabriel

Mercury: Raphael

Venus: Anael

Mars: Samael

Jupiter: Sachiel

Saturn: Cassiel

Uranus: Uriel

Neptune: Asariel

Pluto: Azrael

In the Kabbalah, ten archangels are responsible for the ten sephiroth in the Tree of Life. They are:

Kether (Crown): Metatron

Chokmah (Wisdom): Raziel

Binah (Understanding): Zaphkiel

Chesed (Mercy): Zadkiel

Geburah (Strength): Samael

Tiphereth (Beauty): Michael

Netzach (Victory): Haniel

Hod (Splendor): Raphael

Yesod (Foundation): Gabriel

Malkuth (Kingdom): Sandalphon and Uriel

Zoroastrianism has six or seven archangels, known as the Immortal Holy Ones. The confusion about the exact number is because of Ahura Mazda, or "Wise Lord." He is believed to be the architect of everything that is good in the world. Some people consider him to be an archangel, while others believe that he is God. Here are the six who are considered to be archangels:

1. Vohu Manah, or "Perfect Mind," provides enlightenment and also welcomes the souls of the righteous when they first arrive in heaven.

2. Asha, or "Righteousness," is the healing angel. He also teaches spiritual values.

3. Khshathra Vairya, or "Dreams Fulfilled," is in charge of prosperity and any matters concerning the material world.

4. Spenta Armaiti, or "Holy Devotion," is a female archangel. She is the earth spirit who provides nurturing, love, and forgiveness.

5. Haurvatat, or "Perfection," provides protection. He works closely with Ameretat.

6. Ameretat, or "Immortality," ensures that the worthy move on to the next level after this incarnation.

The variety and number of archangels has kept angelologists busy for at least two thousand years. Here are some of the better-known archangels.

Anael

Anael (Hamiel, Hanael, Onoel) is considered the prince of archangels, and was one of the seven angels of Creation. He is the archangel who appeared to Barnabas Saul when he was scrying for Dr. John Dee. Anael is responsible for the planet Venus, and plays a major role in human love and sexuality. He is also involved with beauty, the arts, and nature. He rules the second heaven, and receives the prayers that ascend from the first heaven. Anael rules Friday.

Archangel of Right Thinking

The Archangel of Right Thinking, who is about nine times the size of a human being, is credited with bringing Zoroaster into the presence of God. Virtually nothing is known about this archangel. However, his actions helped establish Zoroastrianism. The thirty-year-old Zoroaster immediately began work on his new religion, aided by the Immortal Holy Ones, the six archangels who were dedicated to helping him.

Azrael

Azrael means "whom God helps." He lives in the third heaven and records the names of people when they are born, and erases them once they die. He is related to the planet Pluto, and is interested in death, reincarnation, and the occult. In Jewish and Islamic lore, Azrael is considered the angel of death.

Barakiel

Barakiel means "lightning of God." Not surprisingly, Barakiel rules thunder and lightning. Along with Uriel and Rubiel, Barakiel is invoked for success in gambling.

Cassiel

Cassiel is the ruler of Saturn, the planet of restriction and limitations. Consequently, he is known as the angel of solitude and tears. Cassiel teaches people to stand on their own two feet, and to take charge of their lives. He has an interest in inheritances, wills, agriculture, and long-term illnesses. As Saturn is a slow-moving planet, any petitions to Cassiel take time to be answered. Cassiel rules Saturday.

Chamuel

Chamuel (Camael, Camiel, Kemuel) means "he who seeks God" or "the one who sees God." He is the archangel of joy, beauty, unconditional love, and all close relationships. Chamuel and Gabriel are believed to be the angels who gave Jesus strength in the Garden of Gethsemane.

Chamuel is the ruler of Mars, which gives him a fiery, warlike disposition. However, he is also in charge of the singing in heaven. Consequently, he has had a mixture of positive and negative qualities assigned to him. Enoch wrote that he was one of God's favorite angels. Chamuel provides courage, strength, assertiveness, and protection. As long as you are open and honest with him, Chamuel will also help you work on your karma. Chamuel rules Tuesday.

Gabriel

Gabriel means "God is my strength." Gabriel is the angel of purification, guidance, and prophecy. Gabriel looks after heaven, and also intercedes with God on behalf of humanity. Gabriel and Michael are the only two archangels mentioned by name in the Old Testament. Gabriel dictated the

Koran to Muhammad, and is considered by Muslims to be the angel of truth. Gabriel rules Monday. This archangel is covered in much more depth in *Gabriel*, another title in this series.

Israfil

In Muslim lore, Israfil and his helpers will be in charge of the Hour of Judgment Day. Israfil stands at the foot of God's throne, holding the trumpet that he will blow on Judgment Day. In the Christian tradition, Gabriel is the archangel who will perform this task. It is believed that Israfil was Muhammad's companion for three years, and taught him much of what he needed to know to become a prophet. After learning everything he could from Israfil, Gabriel took over as Muhammad's teacher. A well-known Islamic tradition says that Allah sent Gabriel, Michael, Azrael, and Israfil to the four corners of the earth to collect the seven handfuls of dust that were used to create Adam.

Jophiel

Jophiel (or Iophiel or Zophiel) means "the beauty of God." He is the archangel of inspiration, illumination, and wisdom. Not surprisingly, he is also the patron angel of artists. He encourages people to focus on their spiritual nature, and gain enlightenment and understanding. He protects everyone who seeks truth with a humble heart, but is the enemy of those who seek vain knowledge. He is the enemy of pride, ignorance, and bigotry. He is prepared to help you learn and retain information. Consequently, he is often considered to be the guardian of the Tree of Knowledge. According to legend, it was Jophiel who expelled Adam and Eve from the Garden of Eden. He is also believed to have taught the sons of Noah.

Metatron

Some sources place Metatron above all the other archangels. This probably accounts for his name, which means "the throne beside the throne of God." Metatron had an earthly incarnation as the prophet Enoch. He was Adam's great great great great grandson, and was also father of Methusaleh, who became the world's oldest man. Metatron is a teaching angel who now looks after all of mankind. He also keeps the heavenly records, and makes sure that every prayer reaches God. If the prayer is spoken in Hebrew, Metatron asks his twin brother, Sandalphon, for help. The two brothers weave the Hebrew prayer into a garland of flowers that God can wear on his head. In the Kabbalah, he is believed to be the angel who led the children of Israel through the wilderness. Metatron lives in the seventh heaven, and is, for all intents and purposes, God's secretary.

Michael

Michael means "who is like God." Michael is considered the greatest of all the angels in Christianity, Judaism, and Islam.

He is the archangel of truth, integrity, strength, and protection. He and Gabriel are the only two archangels mentioned by name in the Old Testament. He is said to have taught Adam how to grow food from the soil. He is the protector of Israel. In Islam, Michael controls the forces of nature. Michael rules Sunday. Michael is covered in much greater depth in *Michael*, another title in this series.

Raguel

Raguel means "friend of God." Despite this name, Raguel was, along with Uriel and others, rejected at a Church Council in Rome in 745 CE. According to Enoch, Raguel transported him to heaven while he was still a human: "And Enoch walked with God: and he was not; for God took him." (Genesis 4:24) Raguel supervises the behavior of other angels, and disciplines them when necessary. Raguel is known to assist Uriel, and a clue to his areas of interest is that he is sometimes referred to as the angel of ice and snow.

Raphael

Raphael means "God heals," or "the medicine of God." Raphael is the archangel of healing, wholeness, unity, learning, and creativity. He heals the spirit by carrying the prayers of humanity to God. He is first mentioned in the book of Tobit, but is believed to have healed Abraham's circumcision, and the thigh injury that Jacob received from a mysterious, dark assailant at Peniel. He is also generally considered to be the angel who troubled the waters at the healing pool at Bethesda. Raphael rules Wednesday. Raphael is covered in much greater depth in *Raphael,* another title in this series.

Raziel

Raziel means "secret of God." Raziel is one of the nine Briatic archangels in the Kabbalah. He also taught Adam, and is reputed to be the author of the *Sefer Raziel: The Book of the Angel Raziel.* Because of this book, Raziel is referred to as the "Angel of Mysteries," as the book is believed to contain all 1,500 keys to heavenly and earthly knowledge. Tradition says that he gave a copy of his book to Adam and Eve to help them handle life after they were forced out of the Garden of Eden. Apparently, Noah learned how to build the ark after receiving a copy of Raziel's book from Raphael. It would be wonderful if these stories were true. Sadly, that is not the case, as the *Sefer Raziel* dates back only to medieval times. The actual author is unknown.

However, Raziel, the Angel of Mysteries, stands at the curtain that separates God from the rest of creation. As a result, he possesses a huge amount of knowledge that is not known by other angels. Raziel enjoys helping original thinkers with their ideas. Raziel rules the planet Neptune.

Remiel

Remiel is the archangel who guides the souls of the faithful after they have been weighed by Michael. He is also the angel of divine vision, and is willing to help anyone who has a driving need to see what lies ahead.

Sandalphon

Archangel Sandalphon is believed to have originally been the prophet Elijah. He is considered the twin brother of Metatron, who was also human at one time. The name Sandalphon comes from a Greek word that means "co-brother." Sandalphon is believed to be so tall that it would take five hundred years to travel from his feet to the top of his head. His task is to gather up all the prayers of the faithful. He is in charge of karmic debt, and ensures that everything works out over a period of incarnations. He, along with Michael, ceaselessly wages war on Satan.

Sandalphon was also the subject of what is arguably the best-known poem about angels:

Have you read in the Talmud of old,
In the Legends the Rabbins have told
Of the limitless realms of the air,—
Have you read it, —the marvellous story
Of Sandalphon, the Angel of Prayer?

How erect, at the outermost gates
Of the City Celestial he waits
With his feet on the ladder of light,
That, crowded with angels unnumbered,

By Jacob was seen, as he slumbered
Alone in the desert at night?

The Angels of Wind and of Fire
Chant only one hymn, and expire
With the song's irresistible stress;
Expire in their rapture and wonder,
And harp-strings are broken asunder
By music they throb to express.

But serene in the rapturous throng,
Unmoved by the rush of the song,
With eyes unimpassioned and slow,
Among the dead angels, the deathless
Sandalphon stands listening breathless
To sounds that ascend from below;—

From the spirits on earth that adore,
From the souls that entreat and implore
In the fervor and passion of prayer;
From the hearts that are broken with losses,
And weary with dragging the crosses
Too heavy for mortals to bear.

And he gathers the prayers as he stands,
And they change into flowers in his hands,
Into garlands of purple and red;
And beneath the great arch of the portal,
Through the streets of the City Immortal
Is wafted the fragrance they shed . . .

—Henry Wadsworth Longfellow (1807–82),
"Sandalphon," from *Birds of Passage*

Sariel

Sariel works closely with Raguel. His main responsibility is to decide the fate of any angel who strays from the path of righteousness. He is also one of the commanders of God's armies.

Zadkiel

Zadkiel means "righteousness of God." Zadkiel is the angel of mercy, forgiveness, and tolerance. He gives comfort to people who are afraid, and transmutes negative energy into more positive directions. He is considered one of the nine rulers of heaven, head of the fifth heaven, and one of the seven archangels who stand in the presence of God. He is considered the ruler of Jupiter, and possesses all the beneficent qualities of this planet. A Jewish legend says that he was the angel who stopped Abraham from sacrificing his son, Jacob. Consequently, he is usually depicted with a dagger in his right hand. (However, other authorities credit Michael with this.) He and Jophiel are the two standard bearers who are immediately behind Michael when he goes into battle. Zadkiel rules Thursday.

Ten

CONCLUSION

URIEL, Fire of God, is the least known of the archangels of the four directions. However, he is arguably the most popular of all the archangels. This is because of his interests in alchemy and magic, which means that Uriel is invoked more frequently than the others. As you will recall, Uriel is credited with bringing the divine gift of alchemy to humankind. Because of this, alchemists and magicians took a new interest in the angelic realms, and special prayers, rituals, and ceremonies were written to honor Uriel.

In addition to this, Uriel is the archangel people are most likely to call upon when they desperately need help. This is because he is so accessible and amenable to contact. As Uriel is the archangel of ministration and peace, he can take your biggest setbacks and disappointments and turn them into your greatest blessings.

Uriel has suffered as a result of not being mentioned by name in the Bible. However, his loyalty to God is undeniable, which is why he stands guard at the gates of hell. This is part of his ceaseless battle against evil. Uriel is the bringer of divine vengeance and justice, but he is also the archangel who will bring you the peace "which passeth all understanding," if you let him. Never forget that Uriel provides the flame of pure love. That is his greatest gift to humanity.

I hope this book will enable you to welcome him into your life.

Notes

Introduction

1. "To My Friend on the Death of His Sister," by John Greenleaf Whittier.

2. Pseudo-Dionysius, *Pseudo-Dionysius: The Complete Works,* translated by Colm Luibheid (New York: Paulist Press, 1987), 160–61.

3. Harvey Humann, *The Many Faces of Angels* (Marina del Rey, CA: DeVorss Publications, 1986), 88.

4. In one of his books, Emanuel Swedenborg wrote that angels enjoyed all of the earthly pleasures, such as eating, reading, and making love, in heaven (Emanuel Swedenborg, *The Essential Swedenborg,* selected and edited and with an introduction by Sig Synnestvedt [New York: The Swedenborg Foundation, 1970], 104–18). However, in another book, he claims that angels are etheric, rather than physical, beings (Emanuel Swedenborg, *Angelic*

Wisdom Concerning Divine Love and Wisdom, translated by John C. Ager [New York: Citadel Press, Inc., 1965], 88–89).

5. Karl Barth, *Church Dogmatics, Volume 3, Part 3*, translated by G. W. Bromiley and R. J. Ehrlich (Edinburgh, Scotland: T. & T. Clark, 1960), 486.

6. Geddes MacGregor, *Angels: Ministers of Grace* (New York: Paragon House, 1988), 57.

Chapter One

1. Louis Ginzberg, *The Legends of the Jews,* chapter V (Philadelphia, PA: The Jewish Publication Society of America, 1925), 125.

2. Joel, *Chronographia,* edited by Immanuel Bekker (Bonn, Germany: Impensis E. Weberi, 1836), 3. Joel was a twelfth-century Byzantine historian.

3. Louis Ginzberg, *The Legends of the Jews,* chapter IV (Philadelphia, PA: The Jewish Publication Society of America, 1913), 356–57.

4. The second book of Esdras is also known as the fourth book of Ezra and *Ezra Apocalypse*. The main part of the work was originally written in Aramaic by an unknown author in about 100 CE. In about 250 CE, two new chapters were added to the Greek translation of the manuscript, and one hundred years after that, someone added the final

two chapters. It was later printed as an appendix to the New Testament in the Latin Vulgate Bible.

5. The *Sibylline Oracles* are a collection of prophecies in verse that were allegedly written by a Greek prophetess (sibyl) to confirm a number of Jewish and Christian teachings. They were probably the work of a number of Jewish and Christian writers between 150 BCE and 189 CE. The manuscript originally contained fifteen books, but numbers nine, ten, and fifteen are lost.

6. John Milton, *Paradise Lost*, books 3–5. First published in 1667. Many editions available.

7. Francis Barrett, *The Magus*, page 56. First published in 1801. Many editions available. Mine is a facsimile edition published by the Aquarian Press, Wellingborough, UK, in 1989.

8. Francis Barrett, *The Magus* (1801; reprint, Wellingborough, UK: Aquarian Press, 1989), 57.

9. Peter French, *John Dee: The World of an Elizabethan Magus* (New York: Ark Paperbacks, 1972), 28. See also Julian Roberts and Andrew G. Watson, eds., *John Dee's Library Catalogue* (London: Bibliographical Society, 1990).

10. John Dee, *Mysteriorum Liber Primus*, BL MS Sloane 3188.

11. This quote comes from John Dee's diary of December 22, 1581. There have been several editions of John Dee's diaries, including James O. Halliwell, ed., *The Private Diary of John Dee*, vol. XIX, (London: Camden Society Publications, 1842); John E. Bailey, ed., *Diary for the Years 1595–1601* (privately printed, 1880); and Edward Fenton, ed., *The Diaries of John Dee* (Charlbury, Oxon., 1998). More accessible is a work in progress on the Internet called *The John Dee Publication Project,* http://www.john-dee.org, which intends to ultimately publish all of John Dee's diaries.

12. John Dee's diary, December 22, 1581.

13. John Dee's diary, March 10, 1582.

14. John Dee's diary, March 10, 1582.

15. John Dee's diary, March 11, 1582.

16. The communications that John Dee and Edward Kelley received included *de Heptarchia Mystica* (Mysteries of the Sevenfold Kingdom), *Liber Logaeth* (Book of the Speech of God), *The Round Tablet of Nalvage, 48 Claves Angelicae* (Book of the Forty-Eight Angelic Keys), *Liber Scientiae Auxilii et Victoriae Terrestris* (Book of Knowledge, Help, and Earthly Victory), and *The Book of Supplications and Invocations.*

17. John Dee's diary, May 5, 1583.

18. Colin Wilson, *The Occult: A History* (London, UK: Hodder & Stoughton, Ltd., 1971), 273–74.

19. John Dee's crystal ball, or "shew-stone," as he called it, and magic mirror can be seen in the Department of Medieval and Later Antiquities (Room 44) in the British Museum in London. His magical table, which was heavily inscribed with occult symbols, can be seen at the Ashmolean Museum in Oxford, UK.

20. Corinne Heline, *The Blessed Virgin Mary* (New York: New Age Press, 1971), 110.

21. Charles Lamb, quoted in *The Oxford Book of the Supernatural*, edited by D. J. Enright (Oxford, UK: Oxford University Press, 1994), 196.

22. William G. Gray, *The Ladder of Lights* (York Beach, ME: Samuel Weiser, 1981), 88. Originally published in 1968 by Helios Book Service, Ltd., Cheltenham, UK.

Chapter Two

1. Dion Fortune, *Guild of the Master Jesus.* Essay included in *The Story of Dion Fortune* by Charles Field and Carr Collins (Dallas, TX: Star & Cross Publication, 1985), 283.

Chapter Three

1. An oracle tree is part of the Celtic tradition. It is a tree that you develop a special bond with. Most people find their oracle trees by hugging different trees until they find one that responds well to them. Over a period of time, the relationship between the person and the tree grows, and often the person will look after the area in the vicinity of the tree, taking care of any fauna and flora that are closeby. Oracle trees are particularly good places to rest, meditate, think, communicate with the angelic kingdom, and perform magic. See Richard Webster, *Omens, Oghams & Oracles* (St. Paul, MN: Llewellyn Publications, 1995), 39–41.

Chapter Four

1. Irenaeus, *Patrologia cursus completus Graeca* (Paris: Garnier Fratres, 1857), volume 8.

2. Udo Becker, *The Continuum Encyclopedia of Symbols,* translated by Lance W. Garmer (New York: Continuum, 1994), 257. Originally published in Germany by Verlag Herder Freiburg im Breisgau, 1992.

3. *Encyclopaedia Britannica, Micropaedia,* 15th edition, volume VII (Chicago, IL: Encyclopaedia Britannica, Inc., 1983), 308.

Chapter Five

1. *Encyclopaedia Britannica, Micropaedia,* 15th edition, volume VII (Chicago, IL: Encyclopaedia Britannica, Inc., 1983), 691.

2. Geoffrey Keyte, *The Mystical Crystal* (Saffron Walden, UK: C. W. Daniel Co., 1993), 51.

3. Onomacritis, quoted in *Precious Stones and Gems* by Edwin W. Streeter (London: Chapman and Hall, Ltd., 1877), 17.

4. Richard Cavendish, ed., *Man, Myth & Magic,* volume 6 (London: Marshall Cavendish, Ltd., 1985), 1510.

5. John Sinkankis, *Emerald and Other Beryls* (Prescott, AZ: Geoscience Press, 1989), 73.

6. George Frederick Kunz, *The Curious Lore of Precious Stones* (Philadelphia, PA: J. B. Lippincott Co., 1913), 61.

7. Bernardino de Sahagun, quoted in William Jones, *History and Mystery of Precious Stones* (London: Richard Bentley and Son, 1880), 29.

8. George Frederick Kunz, *The Curious Lore of Precious Stones,* 64.

9. Cardano, quoted in *The Curious Lore of Precious Stones* by George Frederick Kunz, 52.

10. George Frederick Kunz, *The Magic of Jewels and Gemstones* (Philadelphia, PA: J. B. Lippincott Co., 1915), 57.

11. Richard Webster, *How to Give Readings with Gemstones* (Albuquerque, NM: Flora and Company, 1993).

12. Hobrin, *Gemstone Reading for Profit* (Auckland, NZ: Brookfield Press, 1988).

Chapter Seven

1. Arthur Edward Waite, *The Book of Ceremonial Magic* (London: William Rider and Son, Ltd., 1911), 97.

2. Donald Tyson, *Scrying for Beginners* (St. Paul, MN: Llewellyn Publications, 1997), 133.

Chapter Nine

1. There are many different listings of archangels, including the following: *The Testament of Solomon* lists Mikael, Gabriel, Uriel, Sabrael, Arael, Iaoth, and Adonael. Pope Gregory the Great (540–604) listed Michael, Gabriel, Raphael, Uriel, Simiel, Orifiel, and Zachariel. Pseudo-Dionysius listed Michael, Gabriel, Raphael, Uriel, Chamuel, Jophiel, and Zadkiel. *The Hierarchy of Blessed Angels* lists Raphael, Gabriel, Chamuel, Michael, Adabiel, Haniel, and Zaphiel. The first book of Enoch lists

Uriel, Raphael, Raguel, Michael, Zerachiel, Gabriel, and Remiel.

2. Francis Barrett, *The Magus* (1801; reprint, Wellingborough, UK: Aquarian Press, 1989), 104.

Suggested Reading

Apocrypha. *The Books Called Apocrypha According to the Authorized Version*. London: Oxford University Press, n.d.

Auerbach, Loyd. *Psychic Dreaming: A Parapsychologist's Handbook*. New York: Warner Books, 1991.

Black, Matthew, commentator and editor. *The Book of Enoch, or, 1 Enoch: A New English Edition*. Written in consultation with James C. VanderKam. Leiden, Netherlands: E. J. Brill, 1985.

Brandon, S. G. F. *Religion in Ancient History*. London: Allen & Unwin, 1973.

Brockington, L. H. *A Critical Introduction to the Apocrypha*. London: G. Duckworth, 1961.

Bunson, Matthew. *Angels A to Z*. New York: Crown Trade Paperbacks, 1996.

Cunningham, Scott. *Earth Power*. St. Paul, MN: Llewellyn Publications, 1983.

————. *Earth, Air, Fire & Water*. St. Paul, MN: Llewellyn Publications, 1991.

Davidson, Gustav. *A Dictionary of Angels, Including the Fallen Angels*. New York: Free Press, 1967.

Fox, Matthew, and Sheldrake, Rupert. *The Physics of Angels: Exploring the Realm Where Science and Spirit Meet*. San Francisco, CA: HarperSanFrancisco, 1996.

French, Peter. *John Dee: The World of an Elizabethan Magus*. New York: Ark Paperbacks, 1972.

Ginzberg, Louis. *The Legends of the Jews (7 volumes)*. Translated by Henrietta Szold. Philadelphia, PA: The Jewish Publication Society of America, 1909–38.

Giovetti, Paola. *Angels: The Role of Celestial Guardians and Beings of Light*. Translated by Toby McCormick. York Beach, ME: Samuel Weiser, 1993.

González-Wippler, Migene. *Return of the Angels*. St. Paul, MN: Llewellyn Publications, 1999.

Hodson, Geoffrey. *The Angelic Hosts*. London: The Theosophical Publishing House, 1928.

Jones, Timothy. *Celebration of Angels*. Nashville, TN: Thomas Nelson Publishers, 1994.

Kabbani, Muhammad Hisham. *Angels Unveiled: A Sufi Perspective*. Chicago, IL: Kazi Publications, 1995.

Knight, Christopher, and Lomas, Robert. *Uriel's Machine*. Gloucester, MA: Fair Winds Press, 1999.

Milik, J. T., ed. *The Books of Enoch: Aramaic Fragments of Qumrân Cave 4.* Oxford, UK: Oxford University Press, 1976.

Moolenburgh, H. C. *A Handbook of Angels.* Translated by Amina Marix-Evans. Saffron Walden, UK: C. W. Daniel, 1984.

Myer, Isaac. *Qabbalah: The Philosophical Writings of Solomon ben Yehudah Ibn Gebirol, or Avicebron.* 1888. Reprint, London, UK: Robinson and Watkins, 1972.

Palmer, Lynn. *A Beginner's Guide to Angels.* London: Hodder & Stoughton, Ltd., 1999.

Parrinder, Edward Geoffrey. *Worship in the World's Religions.* London: Faber & Faber, 1961.

Pseudo-Dionysius. *Pseudo-Dionysius: The Complete Works.* Translated by Colm Luibheid. New York: Paulist Press, 1987.

RavenWolf, Silver. *Angels: Companions in Magic.* St. Paul, MN: Llewellyn Publications, 1996.

Ringgren, Helmer. *Israelite Religion.* Translated by David E. Green. Philadelphia, PA, Fortress Press, 1966.

Shinners, John, ed. *Medieval Popular Religion 1000–1500: A Reader.* Orchard Park, NY: Broadview Press, 1997.

Swedenborg, Emanuel. *Heaven and Hell.* Translated by George F. Dole. West Chester, PA: Swedenborg Foundation, 1976.

Sweetman, James Windrow. *Islam and Christian Theology (4 volumes)*. London: Lutterworth Press, 1947.

Turner, Robert, ed. *The Heptarchia Mystica of John Dee*. Wellingborough, UK: Aquarian Press, 1986.

Tyson, Donald. *Enochian Magic for Beginners*. St. Paul, MN: Llewellyn Publications, 1997.

Webster, Richard. *Spirit Guides & Angel Guardians*. St. Paul, MN: Llewellyn Publications, 1998.

Woolley, Benjamin. *The Queen's Conjurer*. London: Harper-Collins, 2001.

Index

Grace your bookshelves
with the extraordinary Archangel series
by Richard Webster

The archangels—Michael, Gabriel, Raphael, and Uriel—
are a powerful source of inspiration and enlightenment.
Each book in this series offers real-life angel stories from
the Richard Webster's own experiences, and a variety of
methods for connecting with each archangel, petitioning
his or her help, and creating a lasting bond.

Series titles:

Michael
Communicating with the Archangel for
Guidance & Protection
0-7387-0540-3 • $11.95

Gabriel
Communicating with the Archangel for
Inspiration & Reconciliation
0-7387-0641-8 • $10.95

Raphael
Communicating with the Archangel for
Healing & Creativity
0-7387-0649-3 • $11.95

Visit our website at www.llewellyn.com
Or order by phone, toll-free within the U.S.
1-877-NEW-WRLD (1-877-639-9753)

Miracles
Inviting the Extraordinary Into Your Life

RICHARD WEBSTER

A practical guide to creating miracles. Miracles are possible for everyone. Once you understand the nature of the miraculous and start believing in miracles, you can start producing your very own miracles. You can transform your life with the simple steps in this practical how-to guide.

Bestselling author Richard Webster gives you the tools and techniques you need to become a miracle worker. Learn how to perform a powerful, nearly forgotten Hawaiian ritual to achieve your heart's desire, and how to use automatic writing to receive guidance from your higher self. Also covered in this one-of-a-kind handbook are instructions for creating miracles through white magic, creative intuition, chakra energy, and spell casting.

0-7387-0606-X, 288 pp., 5³⁄₁₆ x 8   **$10.95**

Spanish edition
Milagros: De tu diario vivir
0-7387-0618-3, 216 pp., 5³⁄₁₆ x 8, illus.   **$12.95**

To order, call 1-877-NEW-WRLD
Prices subject to change without notice

Angels
Companions in Magick

SILVER RAVENWOLF

Angels do exist. These powerful forces of the Universe flow through human history, riding the currents of our pain and glory. You can call on these beings of the divine for increased knowledge, love, patience, health, wisdom, happiness, and spiritual fulfillment. Always close to those in need, they bring peace and prosperity into our lives.

Here, in this complete text, you will find practical information on how to invite these angelic beings into your life. Build an angelic altar, meet the archangels in meditation, contact your guardian angel, create angel sigils and talismans, work magick with the Angelic Rosary, and talk to the deceased. You will learn to work with angels to gain personal insights and assist in the healing of the planet as well as yourself.

Angels do not belong to any particular religious structure—they are universal. They open their arms to humans of all faiths, bringing love and power into people's lives.

1-56718-724-2, 288 pp., 7 x 10, illus.　　　　　　　**$16.95**

Keys to the Kingdom
Jesus & the Mystic Kabbalah

MIGENE GONZÁLEZ-WIPPLER

Was Jesus a master Kabbalist? Are Jesus' teachings based on Kabbalism? How do the Ten Commandments tie into the Tree of Life? Is the Lord's Prayer a Kabbalist invocation? Migene González-Wippler reveals secrets of the Bible and the life of Jesus in her intriguing introduction to the Christian Kabbalah.

Emphasizing Christian aspects, *Keys to the Kingdom* presents an easy-to-read overview of the Kabbalah, describing its major principles and historical elements. Drawing on the gospels and historical records, González-Wippler examines Jesus as a man and a teacher, providing convincing evidence—based on historical and traditional Jewish law—that Jesus was a master Kabbalist ... as well as the Messiah.

0-7387-0593-4, 240 pp., 6 x 9, illus.   **$12.95**

Spanish edition

Las llaves del reino

0-7387-0648-5, 240 pp., 6 x 9, illus.   **$14.95**

Gnosis of the Cosmic Christ
A Gnostic Christian Kabbalah

TAU MALACHI

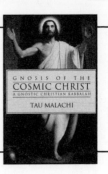

The noble idea of the Christian Kabbalah is not so much the worship of Jesus Christ, but rather a conscious evolution toward a divine or super humanity. In this regard, Christian Kabbalah is quite different from its Jewish roots, and Gnostic Christianity is very different from orthodox Christianity. Both are about experiencing God and evolving toward God, rather than just studying theology.

This groundbreaking work is the first to present the Christian Gnosis of the Kabbalah in a practical and deeply esoteric way. It takes the reader from the basic ideas of the Kabbalah to in-depth explorations of the Tree of Life. Gnostic legends and myths of the Holy Mother, St. Lazarus, St. Mary Magdalene, and Jesus are woven into the study of the Holy Sefirot as well as commentaries on the Ten Commandments and The Beatitudes of the Sermon on the Mount.

0-7387-0591-8, 432 pp., 6 x 9, illus. $19.95

Dowsing for Beginners
The Art of Discovering: Water, Treasure, Gold, Oil, Artifacts

RICHARD WEBSTER

This book provides everything you need to know to become a successful dowser. Dowsing is the process of using a dowsing rod or pendulum to divine for anything you wish to locate: water, oil, gold, ancient ruins, lost objects, or even missing people. Dowsing can also be used to determine if something is safe to eat or drink, or to diagnose and treat allergies and diseases.

Learn about the tools you'll use: angle and divining rods, pendulums, wands—even your own hands and body can be used as dowsing tools! Explore basic and advanced dowsing techniques, beginning with methods for dowsing the terrain for water. Find how to dowse anywhere in the world without leaving your living room, with the technique of map dowsing. Discover the secrets of dowsing to determine optimum planting locations; to monitor your pets' health and well-being; to detect harmful radiation in your environment; to diagnose disease; to determine psychic potential; to locate archeological remains; to gain insight into yourself, and more! *Dowsing for Beginners* is a complete "how-to-do-it" guide to learning an invaluable skill.

1-56718-802-8, 240 pp., 5³⁄₁₆ x 8, illus., photos   **$12.95**

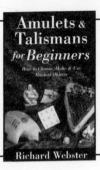

Pendulum Magic
for Beginners
Power to Achieve All Goals

RICHARD WEBSTER

The pendulum is a simple, accurate, and versatile device consisting of a weight attached to a chain or thread. Arguably the most underrated item in the magician's arsenal, the pendulum can reveal information not found any other way. It can read energy patterns, extracting information from deep inside our subconscious.

This book will teach you how to perform apparent miracles such as finding lost objects, helping your potted plants grow better, protecting yourself from harmful foods, detecting dishonesty in others, and even choosing the right neighborhood. Explore past lives, recall dreams, release blocks to achieving happiness, and send your wishes out into the universe.

0-7387-0192-0, 288 pp., 5³⁄₁₆ x 8, illus.   **$13.95**

Candle Magic for Beginners

RICHARD WEBSTER

Anyone who has made a wish before blowing out birthday candles has practiced candle magic. Quick, easy, and effective, this magical art requires no religious doctrine or previous magic experience. Anyone can practice candle magic and Richard Webster shows you how to get started. Learn how to perform rituals, spells, and divinations to gain luck, love, prosperity, protection, healing, and happiness. Also included are tips for which kinds of candles to use, candle maintenance and preparation, best times for magic, and how to make your own candles.

0-7387-0535-7, 312 pp., 5³⁄₁₆ x 8   **$13.95**

Spanish edition
Velas mágicas para principiantes
0-7387-0647-7, 264 pp., 5³⁄₁₆ x 8   **$12.95**